Coral, Conservation, & Careers

50 Ways To Save The Reefs!

Book edited by

Marissa Kempf

First printing edition 2024.

MarineScienceOdyssey.org

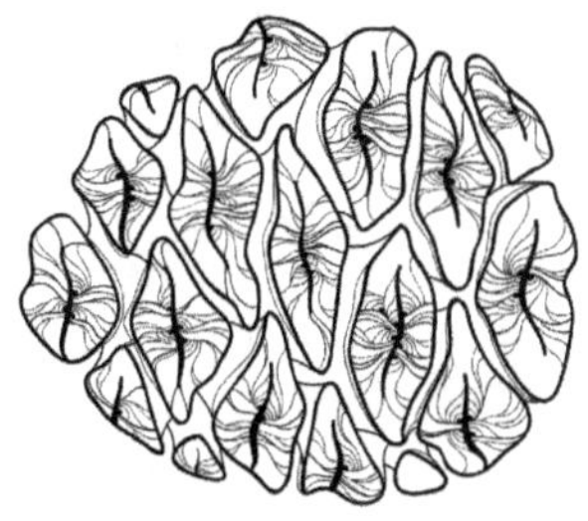

This book is dedicated to all who share a passion for saving the reefs and creating healthier oceans.

Table of Contents

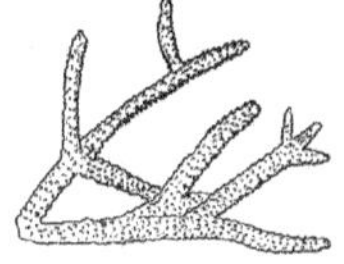

Foreword

When Scott approached me to write this foreword, I was eager to read this guide and lend support for another of his great marine education products.

This is an easy-to-read handbook for anyone looking to get more involved in coral reef conservation. It highlights the importance of coral reefs and gives readers options ranging from outreach to volunteerism to preparing for a career in marine conservation. Growing up, I spent a lot of time poking around in tide pools, collecting shells on beaches, and snorkeling around coral reefs, never imagining that there were careers I could have protecting these amazing places. I wish I had a guide like this when I was in high school, when I was preparing for my lifetime career of protecting the ocean!

As the threats to coral reefs increase, it is more important now than ever to get engaged in saving these incredibly beautiful and valuable ecosystems.

I am excited to see how this guide generates more interest and commitment to coral conservation!

Jennifer Koss

NOAA Coral Reef Conservation Program Director

How to Use This Guide Book

Our goal is to produce books that combine creativity, extra resources and places to take notes for a more powerful learning experience. This book is designed to be an interactive guide to help your coral restoration and conservation journey be easier, rewarding and fun.

This book is more than just a guide; it's a hands-on experience designed to inspire creativity, enhance learning, and motivate action. Whether you're using it for sketching and coloring, note taking, brainstorming, or for the QR Codes sending you to extra resources, it offers multiple ways for you to engage with and support coral conservation. Here's how to make the most of them.

50 Options!

This book offers 50 different ways for you to get involved in coral restoration and conservation efforts. These topics range from simple actions for people that don't know where to start to more involved topics for people that are on their conservation journey already. These practical topics empower you to make a positive impact on coral conservation, whether you're a beginner or an experienced environmental advocate. This guide is your navigational chart to action, providing numerous ideas to contribute to the protection and restoration of coral reefs.

QR Codes

In addition to the topics discussed in this book you will find many QR codes that serve as portals to deeper knowledge. Each code leads to more resources, such as articles, directories or even opportunities for volunteering, interning and more. By scanning these QR codes, you can dive deeper into the world of coral conservation, making this book not only a creative tool but also an educational resource. It allows you to learn at your own pace and explore various aspects of marine science with just a scan of your phone or tablet. It also allows us to maintain ever-expanding resources without constantly having to edit and republish this book.

Notes

A notes section is included for every topic covered in the book, providing space for personal reflections, observations, or anything else you'd like to remember. We want to encourage you to engage with the material more actively, creating a more rewarding personal learning journey. You can jot down key facts, thoughts, or questions that arise as you explore the world of coral restoration, keeping track of your progress and expanding your understanding over time. The notes section makes this book a valuable map for your ongoing exploration.

Sketching & Coloring

Have fun and be creative! There are basic sketches throughout this book for you to color and add to with your own sketches. We hope that you connect with marine life in a fun and artistic way. These simple illustrations of corals give you the freedom to express your creativity while learning about coral reefs. Coloring and adding to the sketches can be a relaxing and engaging way to help get your creativity flowing.

So - this book is more than just a guide; it's a hands-on experience designed to inspire creativity, enhance learning, and motivate action. Whether you're using it as a sketchbook, a journal, a study guide, or a tool for action, it offers multiple ways for you to engage with and support coral restoration and conservation. We have assembled 50 ways to get involved and you only need to choose one to start making a difference. We like those odds! So, let's dive in and get you on your way!

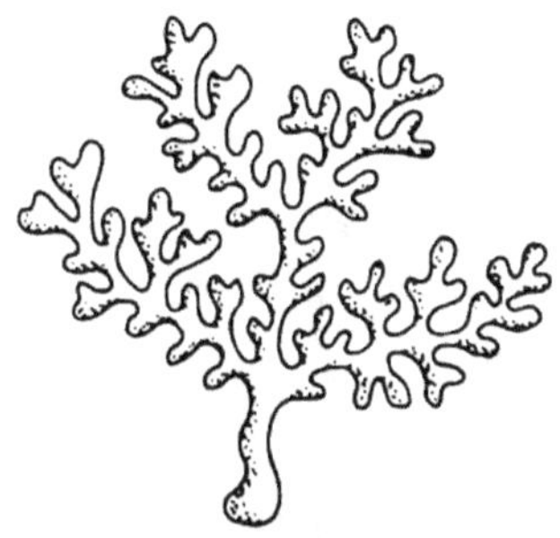

Introduction

Our planet is covered by 71% of oceans, yet we have explored more in outer space than our deep blue oceans. Coral reefs are a very important ecosystem living in our oceans that are rapidly declining, and they need our help. Welcome to Marine Science Odyssey. We are a non-profit dedicated to ocean conservation and guiding everyday people on ways they too can help our oceans.You don't have to be a scientist, SCUBA diver, live near an ocean, or know how to swim to help our coral reefs. This book will take you on a voyage of coral restoration and help you navigate the many ways to get involved. Whether you live near an ocean, in a landlocked state, or on top of a mountain, there are ways you can help. We invite you to come along on this journey of coral restoration and the exciting ways you can make a difference.

Coral reefs are more than just beautiful underwater landscapes. They provide critical ecosystem services to both marine and human communities. Coral reefs are often referred to as the "rainforests of the sea" due to their rich biodiversity and the oxygen they produce for our planet.

They are home to a vast array of marine species, acting as nurseries and feeding grounds. Coral reefs provide livelihoods for millions of people around the world through fishing and tourism industries. Coral reefs also act as our natural barriers at sea against storms, large waves, and protecting our coastlines from erosion.

Unfortunately, coral reefs are under severe threat. Human activities such as coastal development, pollution, overfishing, and especially climate change have led to widespread coral bleaching, coral disease, and the destruction of our coral reefs. By restoring damaged reefs, coral restoration efforts aim to reverse some of the harm caused by these stressors, giving coral populations a chance to recover and thrive. Time is of the essence, so volunteers like you and I play a key role in restoring coral reefs. We are needed all over the world to help revive coral reefs. Your passion, dedication, and willingness to get involved are invaluable to the success of coral restoration projects, so we encourage you to help make a difference.

One of the primary benefits of coral restoration is the enhancement of biodiversity. Coral reefs act as a nursery and provide habitats for numerous species of fish of all ages, invertebrates, and other marine organisms. Through replanting orals in degraded reef areas, restoration projects help reestablish the structural complexity of reefs, which is essential for these species. As the coral colonies grow, they create more space for marine life, which in turn helps restore the intricate web of ecological interactions that coral reefs support. This not only benefits marine biodiversity but also contributes to the stability and health of entire ocean ecosystems.

Another way coral restoration aids in conservation is by promoting resilience to climate change. In some restoration projects, scientists are planting heat-resistant coral species or selectively breeding corals that can tolerate higher ocean temperatures. These efforts aim to enhance the overall resilience of coral populations to climate-induced stressors such as warming oceans and acidification. By focusing on corals with stronger genetic traits, these projects hope to create reefs that are better able to survive in changing environmental conditions and thereby supporting long-term conservation goals.

Coral restoration also contributes to the economic sustainability of coastal communities. Healthy coral reefs are essential to industries such as tourism and fishing, both of which provide livelihoods for millions of people globally. Restoring coral reefs helps ensure that these communities continue to benefit from the ecosystem services provided by healthy reefs, such as food sources and income from tourism. Additionally, coral reefs offer natural protection against coastal erosion and storm surges, further supporting the well-being of these communities.

Coral restoration also fosters community engagement and public awareness. Many restoration projects involve local communities, volunteer divers, and scientists working together to grow and transplant corals. This not only increases the manpower available for restoration but also educates the public about the importance of coral conservation. By actively participating in these efforts, individuals and communities become more invested in protecting their local marine environments, which can lead to stronger, more widespread conservation efforts.

It's important to understand that coral restoration is a powerful tool in the broader effort to conserve coral reefs. It helps rebuild damaged ecosystems, enhances biodiversity, strengthens resilience to climate change, supports the livelihoods of coastal communities, and fosters environmental stewardship. Through these combined benefits, coral restoration plays an integral part in ensuring the survival of coral reefs for future generations.

Notes, Thoughts, Ideas, etc.

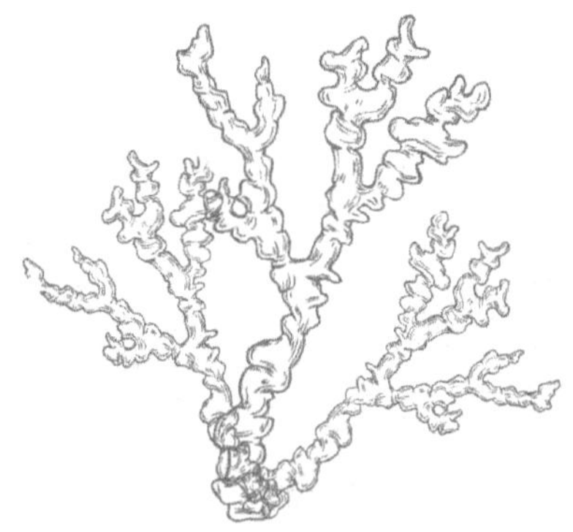

Chapter One
Volunteering

Coral restoration is a growing environmental effort that seeks to rehabilitate damaged coral reefs, which are vital ecosystems under threat from climate change, pollution, and human activities. These underwater gardens are essential to marine life and have far-reaching impacts on the environment and coastal communities. But did you know that volunteers, everyday people like you and me, are at the heart of this movement?

So you may ask yourself how coral restoration actually works? Coral restoration involves the active intervention and assistance in the regrowth and regeneration of coral reefs. Corals are grown in land based and ocean nurseries. Next, these healthy coral fragments are planted onto dead coral heads and in damaged reef areas. These outplants are continuously monitored for growth, disease, overgrowth of algae, and predators such as the yellow tongue snail. The goal is to help these ecosystems recover from damage and boost their natural ability to thrive and restore biodiversity and marine life to our oceans.

Coral restoration is labor-intensive, requiring a lot of manpower to plant and monitor coral fragments. Without the support of volunteers, many projects would lack the resources to make a meaningful impact. Volunteers participate in activities like coral gardening, where baby corals are nurtured and grown until they are ready to transplant onto our reefs.This includes monitoring water quality, controlling algae growth, and giving these coral babies a controlled environment to thrive in. Once these coral fragments are ready to be planted into the wild, volunteers assist in monitoring reef health and contribute to data collection for research. These activities enable coral reefs to grow and recover much faster than they would naturally.

Most coral restoration projects do not require specialized skills, although some basic knowledge of marine ecosystems or diving certifications can be beneficial. Volunteers may receive training on-site to prepare for specific tasks, from underwater work to data entry for scientific purposes. It's also a deeply rewarding experience that allows participants to form connections with like-minded individuals, gain hands-on conservation experience, and witness the beauty of restored reefs firsthand.

There are several ways to contribute to coral restoration, depending on your location, skills, and available time. In this chapter we list 10 ways you can volunteer and help make a difference. Keep in mind that there are different requirements depending on the organization, their location, and whether there are fees incorporated in their volunteering opportunities.

Make sure to use the QR code to learn more about volunteering in coral restoration conservation. We have volunteering resources around the world to help you find the perfect fit. So let's get started with some Volunteering Topics…

Notes, Thoughts, Ideas, etc.

Marine Science Organizations

Volunteering with a Marine Science Organization, even if it's not directly involved in coral restoration activities, can still offer significant opportunities to make a meaningful impact on marine conservation efforts. Many organizations are engaged in critical work like research, education, policy advocacy, and community outreach, all of which play essential roles in protecting the oceans and coral ecosystems. By volunteering, you contribute to raising awareness, supporting scientific research, or promoting conservation practices, all of which are crucial to preserving marine environments. Even if you've never seen the ocean, your efforts can help shape the way people understand and interact with marine ecosystems, ultimately benefiting coral conservation on a larger scale.

A major benefit of volunteering with such organizations is the chance to build valuable experience that can enhance your future career prospects in coral restoration or marine science. Even though you're not physically restoring reefs, you could be gaining skills in project management, research, data analysis, education, and advocacy which are directly transferable to coral restoration work. These experiences can be excellent additions to your resume, showcasing your commitment and expertise to future employers or academic programs. Demonstrating that you have contributed to marine science in various capacities will make you a stronger candidate for hands-on coral restoration roles when the opportunity arises.

Volunteering also creates connections and friendships with like-minded individuals who share your passion for marine conservation. Even in organizations that aren't focused on coral restoration, you'll be surrounded by people who are committed to protecting the ocean and its inhabitants. These connections can provide valuable networking opportunities, as well as a sense of community and purpose. Over time, these relationships can lead to new opportunities in coral conservation or related fields, as you collaborate with others who may have connections to ocean-based initiatives or projects.

Volunteering with a Marine Science Organization can help feed your passion and purpose. The more you engage with the work, whether it's educating the public about marine life, or supporting scientific research, the more you'll feel connected to the cause. This sense of purpose not only enhances your personal satisfaction but also drives you to stay committed to the long-term goals of marine conservation. Even if you're far from the ocean, your passion and dedication can inspire positive change in the field of coral conservation, while preparing you for future, hands-on roles later in your journey.

Notes, Thoughts, Ideas, etc.

Coral Nurseries

Volunteering with a Coral Nursery Program offers an exciting way to make a direct and meaningful impact on the health of our ocean ecosystems. Coral nurseries are specialized environments where coral fragments are cultivated and grown under controlled conditions before being transplanted back to damaged reefs. As a volunteer, you could have an active role in nurturing these corals, assisting in tasks like maintaining the nursery, cleaning coral fragments, and even helping to transplant them to reef restoration sites. This hands-on experience allows you to be directly involved in the effort to restore coral populations, creating a positive impact in the fight against coral degradation.

One of the benefits of participating with a coral nursery is the chance to learn from marine scientists and experts. Volunteers often work alongside professionals who are conducting cutting-edge research in coral biology, reef restoration, and marine conservation. By joining the program, you not only gain practical skills in coral care and restoration techniques, but you also have the opportunity to deepen your understanding of coral ecosystems. This knowledge can empower you to become a more informed advocate for marine conservation, and it may even inspire future studies or a career in marine science.

In addition to gaining valuable knowledge, volunteering for a coral nursery helps build a strong sense of community and connection. These programs often attract like-minded individuals who are passionate about protecting the environment. Working together toward a common goal creates a collaborative spirit, creating lasting friendships and networks within the conservation community. The experience of restoring corals alongside others who share your commitment to the environment can be incredibly rewarding, providing both personal fulfillment and a sense of accomplishment.

One last thing - volunteering for a coral nursery allows you to contribute to long-term reef conservation efforts. Coral reefs face numerous threats, including climate change, pollution, and overfishing, but efforts like coral nurseries help create more resilient reef systems. By supporting these restoration projects, you are playing an essential role in giving coral ecosystems a chance to recover and thrive. Your work can have lasting positive impacts, contributing to the preservation of coral reefs for future generations and ensuring that these critical habitats continue to support marine biodiversity and coastal communities around the world.

Notes, Thoughts, Ideas, etc.

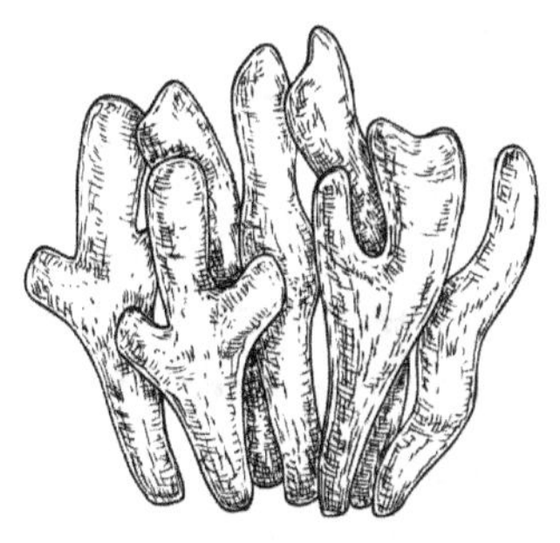

Reef Cleanups

Participating in reef cleanups is a powerful way to contribute to the health of marine ecosystems, whether you're a diver, a non-diver, or even someone living far from the ocean. For divers, reef cleanups provide a hands-on opportunity to directly remove debris that accumulates on coral reefs. Items like plastic bags, fishing gear, single use plastics, and other pollutants can cause significant damage to corals and marine life. By volunteering in underwater cleanup efforts, divers play a crucial role in protecting these ecosystems. Divers must be mindful and trained to ensure they don't accidentally harm fragile coral while removing debris, making this a rewarding but delicate task.

If you're a non-diver but still want to help with reef cleanups, there are many opportunities to participate. You can participate with other snorkelers, removing debris from shallower areas of the reef. You can volunteer and assist the dives when they get back to the docks or the beach. Help them transport the debris, count and document the debris, assist in keeping them hydrated, help the divers sign in or hand out prizes if they have any. These events can be a large undertaking and they definitely could use some help running these important events.

If you live far from the ocean, there are still plenty of ways to get involved in reef cleanups efforts. One way is to support organizations and groups dedicated to reef conservation through donations or advocacy. These organizations often run large-scale cleanup operations, and financial support helps them cover the costs of equipment, volunteer training, and other essential resources. You could also help raise awareness about the importance of reef conservation in your community or through social media and help spread the message. Who knows, you could encourage others who live hundreds of miles away to take action.

You can also contribute by reducing your plastic use and advocating for better waste management practices. Even if you're far from the ocean, the choices you make every day, like using reusable products or supporting businesses with eco-friendly practices, can have a positive impact on coral reefs. Less plastic waste reduces the amount of debris that could potentially make its way into the ocean, protecting marine environments in the long run.

Notes, Thoughts, Ideas, etc.

Community Outreach

Volunteering for coral conservation community outreach is a great way to support the health of our oceans and protect marine ecosystems for future generations. Community outreach programs raise awareness about these issues and inspire collective action. By volunteering, you can contribute to public education, hands-on restoration efforts, and the promotion of sustainable practices, helping to build a movement that prioritizes the protection of coral reefs and the broader marine environment.

One of the key reasons community outreach is important is that it fosters engagement and stewardship. Many people may not fully understand the critical role coral reefs play in supporting marine biodiversity and the health of the planet. Through outreach, you can educate the public, encouraging them to adopt sustainable behaviors and take action to protect reefs. This grassroots engagement creates a ripple effect, where individuals share their knowledge with their communities, driving wider environmental awareness and conservation efforts. It helps build a sense of responsibility and connection to the oceans, ensuring that more people are invested in their preservation.

The rewarding aspect of volunteering for coral restoration outreach lies in the tangible impact you can create. Whether it's through organizing beach cleanups, helping plant coral fragments, or giving educational talks, volunteers contribute directly to the recovery of damaged ecosystems. Your efforts lead to real, measurable improvements in reef health and resilience, which are essential for the survival of numerous marine species. Watching a reef thrive and seeing the results of your work can be incredibly fulfilling, reinforcing the idea that individual actions can make a meaningful difference in environmental conservation.

In addition to making a positive impact on the environment, volunteering for coral restoration community outreach offers personal benefits as well. It provides opportunities for skill development, networking, and personal growth. You will gain hands-on experience in marine science, environmental education, and project management. Working with like-minded individuals, both locally and globally, fosters a sense of community and collaboration, making the experience socially rewarding. These personal and professional growth opportunities make volunteering not only an altruistic endeavor but also an enriching one that can lead to lasting friendships, career advancement, and a deeper connection to the natural world.

Notes, Thoughts, Ideas, etc.

Citizen Science Projects

Joining Citizen Science Projects for coral conservation is a fantastic way to contribute to the protection and restoration of coral reefs, regardless of where you live. These projects enable people from all over the world to participate in real scientific research, helping collect valuable data on coral health, water quality, and marine species populations. Even if you don't live near the ocean, many programs allow you to contribute remotely through online platforms. There are hundreds of ways to participate depending on which project you decide on. By volunteering your time and skills, you play an important role in advancing our understanding of coral ecosystems and their preservation.

If you are living near coastal areas, participating in hands-on Citizen Science Projects can be even more immersive. You might join coral monitoring programs where you snorkel or dive to collect data on coral bleaching, fish populations, or signs of disease. Many organizations will train you to assist in coral planting or reef restoration activities. These projects allow you to directly engage with the marine environment while supporting the work of scientists and conservationists. Being a part of these efforts not only aids coral conservation but also deepens your connection to the natural world and enhances your understanding of marine ecosystems.

If you're not close to the ocean, there are still ways to engage in coral conservation from afar. Many Citizen Science platforms offer virtual projects that involve spreading the word. For example, you could participate in simple programs like posting facts on social media, starting a school conservation club or even doing presentations for local schools and libraries. By providing remote assistance, you help expand the global reach of coral conservation, allowing researchers to cover more ground and gather more data than they could alone. It's a powerful way to make a difference from wherever you are.

In addition to the scientific contributions, joining Citizen Science Projects can also help connect you to the community and collaborate with others. Many programs offer opportunities to connect you with other like-minded individuals who are also passionate about marine conservation. Through online forums, social media groups, and virtual events, you can share experiences, exchange ideas, and stay updated on the latest discoveries in coral conservation. Being part of these networks not only amplifies the impact of your individual efforts but also strengthens global coral conservation movements by creating a shared commitment to protecting these vital ecosystems.

Notes, Thoughts, Ideas, etc.

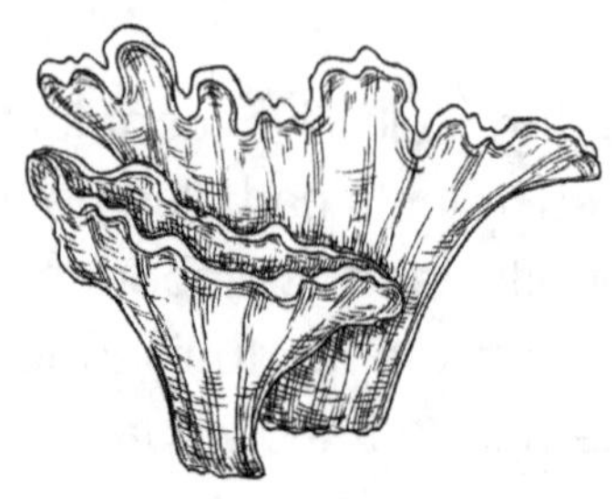

Diver Volunteer

Becoming a dive volunteer for coral restoration and conservation is an exciting way to contribute directly to the protection and recovery of coral reefs. To begin, it's important to have a scuba diving certification, typically through an internationally recognized organization such as PADI, NAUI, or SSI. Coral restoration projects often take place at varying depths, so being a confident, certified diver is essential. Some programs may also require you to have advanced skills or specific certifications in underwater conservation or reef monitoring. Once you have the necessary diving qualifications, you can begin searching for organizations that accept volunteers for coral restoration efforts by using the QR Code at the end of this topic.

Many marine conservation organizations around the world offer opportunities for dive volunteers to actively participate in coral restoration projects. These organizations often run programs where volunteers can help with activities such as planting coral fragments, monitoring reef health, removing invasive species, and cleaning up debris from the ocean floor. Research and choose an organization that aligns with your values and interests, whether it's a local initiative or a global organization. Volunteering can range from short-term projects to longer, more immersive experiences, depending on your availability and commitment.

Before you begin volunteering, most programs will provide training in coral restoration techniques. This training is essential as it teaches you how to handle coral fragments carefully, how to identify different species, and the specific restoration techniques used in that area. These techniques could include coral gardening, attaching coral fragments to artificial reefs, or transplanting corals to degraded areas. Learning these skills ensures that your efforts contribute effectively to the restoration process and help improve the overall health of the reef ecosystem. Training often involves both in-class education and hands-on diving practice.

Being a dive volunteer is not just about underwater work - it's also about cultivating a deeper connection with marine conservation efforts. As a volunteer, you become part of a global community dedicated to saving the world's coral reefs. You'll have the opportunity to learn from marine biologists, conservationists, citizen scientists and local communities. This will help you build a better understanding of the challenges reefs face and the solutions being implemented. Beyond the direct impact on coral health, you'll be advocating for a cause, raising awareness, and inspiring others to take part in the preservation of these vital ecosystems.

Don't live near the ocean? Many people vacation in the Florida Keys specifically to volunteer at one of the many coral restoration projects from Key Largo to Key West. Click the QR Code to learn more.

Notes, Thoughts, Ideas, etc.

Fundraising

Hosting fundraisers for coral conservation efforts can be a great way to raise awareness and support vital marine ecosystems. You can start small with simple, fun, and engaging activities that can be very effective. A bake sale, for example, is an easy way to raise funds while learning about corals. You could bake coral-themed cookies or cupcakes and share facts about the importance of coral reefs with buyers. Another idea could be a "coral art auction," where you and your friends create coral-inspired artwork and invite friends and family to bid on the pieces, turning creativity into a cause.

You can step it up a notch and get more involved in community events like organizing a school-wide "Coral Conservation Day." This could include educational booths, interactive games, and ocean-themed challenges like a sponsored beach or park clean up where participants raise money based on how much debris they gather. You could also collaborate with local marine conservation organizations to arrange guest speakers for your school, giving students an opportunity to learn more about the work being done to protect coral reefs and understand how their fundraiser will help. These activities build a deeper connection to the cause while raising funds and awareness.

Bigger and more elaborate fundraising events can be hosted to target a wider audience. One option is organizing a "Coral Gala," an evening event featuring a formal dinner, live music, guest speakers from marine conservation groups, and a silent auction. Items for auction could include eco-friendly products or experiences, like snorkeling trips to coral reefs or locally crafted artwork inspired by the ocean. This type of event combines education, entertainment, and fundraising, allowing people to engage with the cause while enjoying a memorable evening.

Another idea could be hosting a corporate sponsorship event, such as a harbor clean-up day followed by a fundraising dinner or charity run, where local businesses contribute donations in exchange for publicity and employee participation. Adults can also leverage social media to host virtual fundraisers like livestreamed educational workshops on coral conservation, where viewers donate during the event. These types of fundraisers create larger networks of support, spreading the message far beyond a single event and encouraging ongoing contributions to coral reef protection efforts.

Get creative when thinking of the many ways you can organize a fundraiser to help make an important impact on the coral reefs.

Notes, Thoughts, Ideas, etc.

Beach Patrols

Starting a Beach Patrol for coral conservation is a powerful way to engage the local community and visitors in preserving one of the most vital ecosystems on Earth. The primary mission of the Beach Patrol would be to educate beachgoers about the importance of coral reefs and the simple actions they can take to help protect these delicate habitats. From avoiding harmful sunscreen ingredients to not touching or stepping on coral, the patrol could guide people in adopting reef-friendly practices. Through on-site education, the Beach Patrol would empower individuals to become active participants in marine conservation.

The Beach Patrol would help spread awareness about how everyday actions, such as properly disposing of trash, reducing plastic use, and respecting marine life, can significantly contribute to the health of coral reefs.In addition to its educational role, the Beach Patrol would also foster a sense of responsibility and connection to the ocean. By engaging with volunteers and local citizens, the patrol can create a community of environmentally conscious individuals who are passionate about protecting marine life. The patrol could organize clean-up efforts, lead workshops on marine biology, and involve beachgoers in monitoring water quality and reef health. These hands-on activities not only protect coral reefs but also provide a deeply rewarding experience for those who participate, as they see firsthand the positive impact of their efforts.

The benefits of joining a Beach Patrol extend beyond conservation. Volunteers gain a sense of accomplishment and fulfillment from knowing they are making a difference in protecting the environment. They also develop new skills, learn about marine ecosystems, and form connections with like-minded individuals. The rewarding aspect of contributing to the conservation of coral reefs and the larger ocean ecosystem can be life-changing, fostering a lifelong dedication to preserving the planet's natural resources. Through education, action, and community engagement, a

Beach Patrol could play a pivotal role in safeguarding coral reefs for future generations.

Notes, Thoughts, Ideas, etc.

Social Media

Volunteering through social media to promote coral conservation is a powerful way to spread awareness and engage people in the global effort to protect and restore coral reefs. One of the most direct ways is by sharing content from coral restoration organizations on your own social media platforms. This could include reposting articles, videos, and updates from organizations that you want to volunteer with. By sharing this information with your network, you help raise awareness about the importance of coral reefs and encourage others to support or get involved in conservation efforts.

Another effective method is to create original content that highlights the significance of coral conservation. This could include writing informative posts, making infographics, or creating videos that explain why coral reefs are vital to marine biodiversity and human livelihoods. Highlight specific problems, such as coral bleaching, pollution, or overfishing, and provide actionable steps people can take to help, such as reducing plastic use or supporting coral-friendly businesses. Using relevant hashtags like #CoralConservation, #SaveOurReefs, or #CoralRestoration can help your content reach a broader audience, including people interested in marine conservation.

You can also volunteer by managing social media accounts for coral restoration organizations. Many nonprofits rely on volunteers to handle their social media presence, helping to keep their followers engaged with updates on ongoing projects, fundraising campaigns, and upcoming events. As a social media volunteer, you could help schedule posts, respond to comments, or create campaigns that highlight the progress of coral restoration efforts. This role can be highly impactful, as it keeps the organization's message consistent and ensures that more people are informed about their work.

Starting or participating in online challenges and campaigns can also be an excellent way to generate buzz around coral conservation. You can help launch challenges encouraging people to donate, sign petitions, or commit to sustainable practices like reducing single-use plastics. For example, you might create a "No Plastic for Reefs" challenge, where participants share videos of themselves using reusable bags or bottles, tagging friends to do the same. These interactive campaigns can go viral, bringing attention to the coral conservation movement and motivating others to take action.

Notes, Thoughts, Ideas, etc.

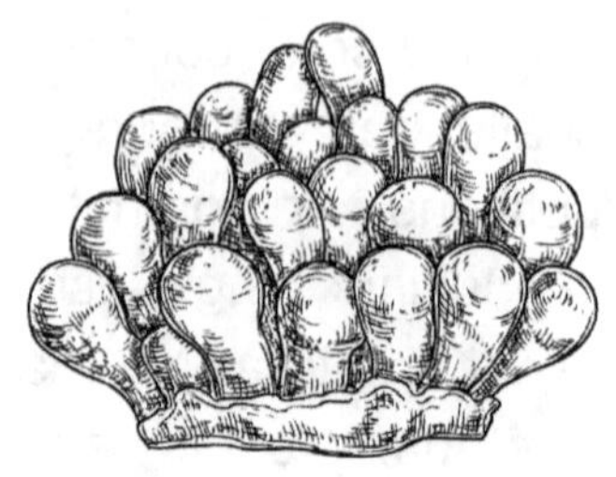

Marine Science Odyssey

Marine Science Odyssey offers a unique opportunity for individuals passionate about ocean conservation to get involved on a global scale. By joining our initiatives, you'll become part of a community dedicated to protecting and restoring coral reefs, which are vital ecosystems for marine life. Whether you're just starting to explore marine science or are looking to deepen your knowledge, Marine Science Odyssey provides countless ways for you to contribute to coral conservation efforts. Volunteering with us allows you to actively participate in spreading their mission of preserving our oceans and ensuring the health of coral reefs worldwide.

One of the greatest advantages of joining Marine Science Odyssey is access to free educational resources. These include articles, webinars, and research materials that cover topics like coral biology, the effects of climate change on marine ecosystems, and the importance of biodiversity. By engaging with this information, you'll not only deepen your understanding of coral conservation but also gain practical knowledge that you can share with others. These educational tools empower our volunteers to become advocates for ocean health, equipping them with the knowledge needed to inspire change in their communities.

In addition to learning through educational content, Marine Science Odyssey offers hands-on experiences through their environmental boot camps. These boot camps provide immersive training in marine science, equipping participants with the skills needed to tackle pressing environmental challenges. You'll learn about restoration techniques, reef monitoring, and sustainable practices that help preserve coral reefs. These experiences foster personal growth and prepare participants to become effective ocean stewards who can contribute to real-world conservation efforts.

By joining Marine Science Odyssey, you'll become part of a global movement focused on protecting our oceans for future generations. Whether you're volunteering your time, engaging in educational opportunities, or attending environmental bootcamps, each step you take will bring you closer to becoming a better steward of the ocean. Together, we can help safeguard coral reefs and ensure the continued health of our marine ecosystems for years to come.

Notes, Thoughts, Ideas, etc.

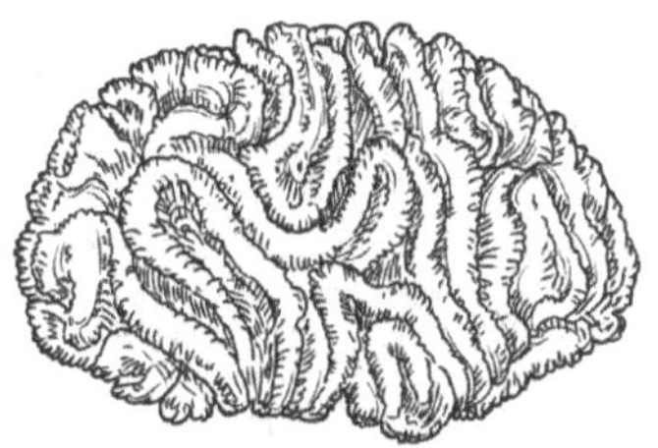

Chapter Two
Internships

Interning with coral restoration organizations is an excellent way to make a meaningful impact on the environment while gaining valuable experience in the field of marine conservation. By interning with organizations dedicated to restoring and preserving these ecosystems, you not only contribute to the health of our oceans but also develop a strong understanding of the complexities involved in coral restoration. This hands-on experience can be a critical stepping stone toward a career in marine biology, environmental science, or conservation.

One of the key benefits of interning with coral restoration organizations is the opportunity to build your resume and develop new skills. Working directly in the field gives you practical experience in coral restoration techniques, data collection, and marine ecology, all of which are highly valued by employers in the environmental and marine science sectors. Moreover, internships often expose you to cutting-edge research and restoration methods, such as coral gardening, outplanting, or monitoring reef health, providing you with a strong technical foundation. Beyond the scientific skills, internships also help you develop soft skills like teamwork, problem-solving, and project management, which are transferable to any career path.

However, interning with coral restoration organizations can be challenging, particularly for those new to the field. Many internships are based in remote or developing areas, where lodging can be hard to find and living conditions might be more basic than what you're used to. You may need to arrange your own accommodation, sometimes sharing spaces with other interns or volunteers. Additionally, many internships offer little to no pay, which can make it difficult to cover living expenses, especially if the program is located far from home. These challenges can be daunting, but they also teach resilience, adaptability, and resourcefulness, qualities that will serve you well in your professional journey.

Despite the challenges, the experience gained from these internships is often highly rewarding. The work you do, from restoring damaged coral reefs to educating local communities about marine conservation, has a direct impact on the health of the oceans. Seeing the fruits of your labor, like coral fragments growing and thriving, or observing fish return to rehabilitated reef areas, can be incredibly fulfilling. It also instills a deep sense of purpose and accomplishment, knowing that you are contributing to the preservation of an ecosystem that supports marine biodiversity and coastal communities worldwide.

In addition to personal fulfillment, interning with a coral restoration organization can set you apart when applying for jobs. Employers in the environmental field highly value candidates with field experience, and coral restoration internships demonstrate a commitment to sustainability and conservation. The hands-on work, scientific knowledge, and problem-solving skills you acquire during the internship will make your resume stand out, especially if you plan to pursue a career in marine biology, environmental consulting, or conservation. Having this unique experience can give you a competitive edge in a job market where practical experience is often just as important as academic qualifications.

While financial constraints and logistical challenges may make interning difficult, there are often scholarships or funding opportunities available to support interns in coral restoration programs. Researching and applying for these can help alleviate some of the financial burden, allowing you to focus more on the experience itself. In some cases, organizations may provide basic lodging or help you find affordable accommodations, and the connections you build with other interns and staff can often lead to shared housing or other solutions.

Perhaps the most significant long-term benefit of interning with coral restoration organizations is the networking opportunities it provides. Working alongside marine scientists, conservationists, and like-minded interns can help you establish professional connections that may lead to future job offers or research opportunities. Interning also gives you a chance to build relationships with mentors who can offer guidance, letters of recommendation, or even help you land your dream job in the marine conservation field.

Ultimately, interning with a coral restoration organization is an experience that can be both challenging and transformative. While it may require sacrifices in terms of comfort and financial stability, the rewards of contributing to the health of coral reefs, gaining invaluable field experience, and building a strong professional network far outweigh the difficulties. For those passionate about marine conservation, it can be a pivotal step toward achieving a fulfilling career and making a lasting difference for our planet's oceans. So let's get started with some Internship topics…

Notes, Thoughts, Ideas, etc.

NOAA (National Oceanic and Atmospheric Administration) Internships

Applying for internships with NOAA's Coral Reef Conservation Program offers an incredible opportunity to gain hands-on experience in one of the most critical areas of marine conservation. As a part of this prestigious government initiative, interns have the chance to work on projects that directly impact the health of coral reefs in U.S. waters and beyond. The program focuses on key aspects of coral restoration, monitoring, and research, allowing you to immerse yourself in activities like coral outplanting, reef health assessments, and community outreach. For those passionate about marine science, this experience is not only rewarding but also a pivotal step toward a career in conservation.

However, securing an internship with NOAA's Coral Reef Conservation Program can be challenging due to the competitive nature of the application process. The program attracts candidates from all over the country, many of whom have strong academic backgrounds and relevant field experience. To stand out, applicants must demonstrate a deep understanding of coral reef ecosystems, strong communication skills, and a commitment to conservation. Interns are often expected to work in demanding environments, both in the field and in research labs, requiring adaptability and resilience. The high level of competition makes these internships in great demand, but being selected is a mark of distinction that will enhance your resume.

Despite the challenges, the perks of interning with NOAA are numerous. Interns have the opportunity to collaborate with leading marine scientists, gain access to cutting-edge research, and contribute to projects with real-world impact. Working with NOAA also provides an insider's view into how government agencies approach large-scale conservation efforts, from policy development to fieldwork. The connections you make during your internship could open doors to future job opportunities, and the mentorship you receive can provide invaluable guidance for your career path. Many NOAA internships also offer stipends or assistance with housing and travel, helping to alleviate some of the financial burdens of interning.

Overall, an internship with NOAA's Coral Reef Conservation Program is a transformative experience that can lead to long-term benefits, both personally and professionally. While the application process is competitive and the work can be challenging, the rewards are worth the effort. You'll gain firsthand experience in coral restoration, develop important skills, and make connections that will support your future career in marine conservation. For those who are passionate about protecting coral reefs and willing to work hard, this is an opportunity that should not be missed.

Notes, Thoughts, Ideas, etc.

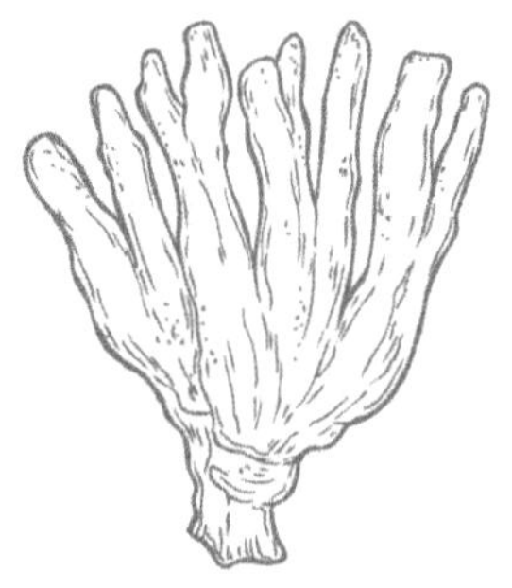

Marine Research Labs

Applying for an internship at a marine research lab that focuses on coral restoration is an incredible opportunity to dive deep into marine science and conservation efforts. These internships are highly rewarding as they allow you to work with leading researchers and participate in groundbreaking coral restoration projects. Interns at marine labs often get hands-on experience with activities like coral propagation, data collection, and reef monitoring, all while learning about the latest scientific techniques used to combat coral decline. The experience you gain in these settings is invaluable and can provide a solid foundation for a career in marine biology or conservation.

Keep in mind, securing an internship at a marine lab can be challenging. Competition is often fierce, especially for well-known labs that offer coral restoration programs, like the Mote Marine Laboratory or research institutes in the Great Barrier Reef. These labs attract applicants from all over the world, many of whom have extensive academic backgrounds or prior experience. To stand out, it's essential to have a strong resume, good references, and a demonstrated passion for marine conservation. Being proactive in seeking out smaller or lesser-known labs can also increase your chances of securing an internship, as these may offer equally rewarding experiences but with less competition.

Marine lab internships are challenging to maintain but come with unique perks and opportunities. Interns often have access to cutting-edge research tools and techniques, as well as the chance to work in breathtaking coastal environments where coral restoration is actively taking place. You may also be involved in fieldwork, spending days on the water collecting samples, conducting underwater surveys, or assisting in coral outplanting efforts. These internships offer the chance to develop close working relationships with leading marine scientists, giving you mentorship opportunities and networking connections that could benefit your future career. Additionally, some programs may provide modest stipends or housing options, helping to offset the financial challenges.

Ultimately, interning at a marine lab for coral restoration is not only a stepping stone toward a career in marine science, but it's also an incredibly rewarding personal experience. You'll be contributing to the preservation of coral reefs, which are vital ecosystems, while learning skills and knowledge that will set you apart in the competitive marine conservation field. Despite the challenges of competition, hard work, and potential financial limitations, the perks of working with passionate professionals and making a tangible impact on coral ecosystems make these internships worthwhile for anyone passionate about marine conservation.

Notes, Thoughts, Ideas, etc.

Eco-volunteering

Eco-volunteering internships abroad offer a unique opportunity to immerse yourself in marine conservation and coral restoration efforts while gaining valuable experience in the field. These internships provide hands-on work in vital conservation activities, such as coral gardening, reef monitoring, and species protection. By participating in these programs, you can develop a wide range of skills that are highly sought after in the environmental and marine science sectors. In addition to scientific and technical expertise, eco-volunteering internships foster problem-solving abilities, cross-cultural communication, and adaptability, which all contribute to building a well-rounded skill set.

One of the greatest benefits of eco-volunteering internships is how they can enhance your resume. Employers in conservation and environmental sciences often seek candidates with real-world experience, and having an internship abroad on your resume shows your commitment to the cause and ability to work in diverse, often challenging environments. The skills you gain from fieldwork, data collection, and working with local communities demonstrate your readiness for a professional career. This kind of practical experience often gives you a competitive edge in job applications, making your resume stand out in a crowded field.

Beyond skill-building, these internships offer the invaluable experience of travel and cultural immersion. Volunteering in a foreign country allows you to engage with different cultures and ecosystems, expanding your understanding of global conservation challenges. Whether you're working in the coral reefs of Fiji, the Caribbean, or Southeast Asia, you'll have the opportunity to explore new environments, meet people from around the world, and learn about conservation efforts in different contexts. Many global efforts practice different coral restoration techniques, so you could gain different skills to expand your knowledge while also being able to contribute that knowledge to other locations.

This experience broadens your worldview while also increasing your cultural sensitivity and global awareness, which can be key in future roles involving international collaboration.

Finally, eco-volunteering internships can lead to personal growth and fulfillment. While the work is often physically and mentally demanding, the reward of knowing you are making a difference in marine conservation is invaluable. As you travel and volunteer abroad, you also build confidence, resilience, and independence—qualities that will serve you well in both your personal and professional life. Overall, eco-volunteering internships offer a meaningful way to combine travel, education, and environmental activism while significantly contributing to your career development.

Notes, Thoughts, Ideas, etc.

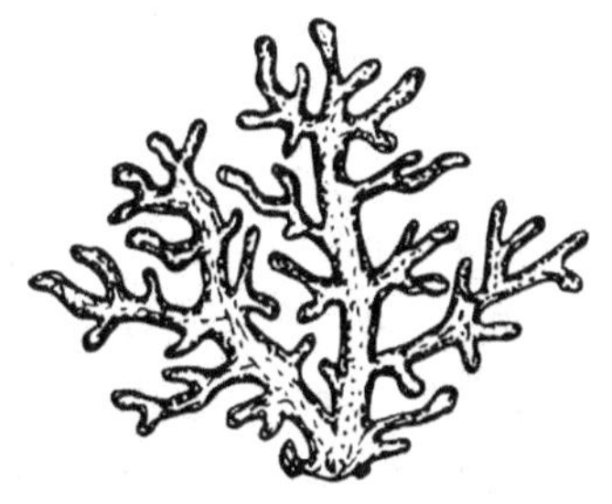

NGOs (Non-Governmental Organizations)

Interning with NGOs like Reef Check or the Coral Triangle Initiative offers you the chance to actively contribute to coral reef conservation. These organizations focus on protecting and restoring coral ecosystems through scientific research, community engagement, and policy advocacy. As an intern, you can work on a variety of projects that involve monitoring reef health, educating communities about sustainable practices, and helping collect data that supports conservation efforts. NGOs often rely on the contributions of passionate volunteers and interns, making them accessible to individuals who may not have formal scientific training but are eager to make a difference.

You can get involved in these internships by applying to programs offered by NGOs that match your interests and skill levels. Many NGOs provide training for their interns, ensuring that even those new to coral conservation can contribute meaningfully. For example, Reef Check offers programs that teach volunteers how to conduct reef surveys and collect data on coral health. These surveys are essential for monitoring reef conditions and informing conservation strategies. Similarly, the Coral Triangle Initiative focuses on working with local communities across Southeast Asia to protect the biodiversity of coral-rich regions, and they welcome interns to assist with public education, project management, and data collection.

Many NGOs offer remote or online internships, allowing individuals to contribute to coral conservation efforts without needing to travel. Remote internships can involve tasks like data analysis, social media management, research assistance, or fundraising efforts. This flexibility makes it possible for people from all over the world to get involved in coral restoration, regardless of their location. By working with NGOs in this capacity, interns can help raise awareness about the importance of coral reefs and engage a wider audience in conservation efforts through online campaigns and outreach.

Your internship with an NGO offers a unique opportunity for personal and professional growth while making a tangible impact on coral conservation. These internships are a great way to gain experience, build skills, and connect with experts in the field of marine conservation. It provides a chance for you to contribute to protecting one of the most vital ecosystems on the planet, and the hands-on experience gained through these internships can also open doors to future careers in environmental science, policy, and advocacy.

Notes, Thoughts, Ideas, etc.

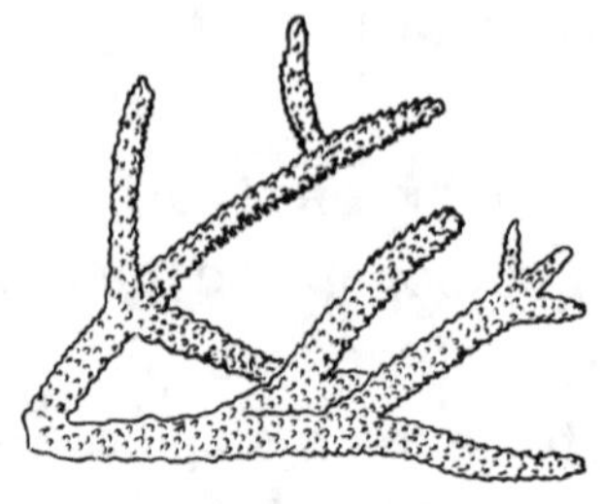

Fieldwork

Fieldwork internships that focus on coral restoration and monitoring offer a unique opportunity to participate directly in hands-on conservation efforts. By interning with local conservation groups, you can contribute to restoring damaged reefs, monitoring coral health, and collecting critical data on the surrounding marine ecosystems. These internships often take place in locations rich in biodiversity, allowing interns to immerse themselves in real-world conservation work. Tasks may include planting coral fragments, assessing reef conditions, removing harmful debris, or even engaging with local communities to raise awareness about coral protection.

One of the major benefits of these fieldwork internships is gaining practical experience. Working directly in the ocean alongside experienced marine biologists and conservationists gives you an understanding of the tools and techniques used in coral restoration, such as coral gardening and transplantation. You'll also learn how to monitor coral health by assessing factors like growth rates, bleaching, and disease, all of which are essential skills in the field of marine biology. This hands-on experience is invaluable for building both technical skills and confidence in conducting scientific research in challenging environments.

Participating in fieldwork internships can also be physically and mentally demanding. The work often takes place in remote coastal regions, requiring you to adapt to unpredictable weather, physical labor, and long hours spent in the water. You may need to manage difficult conditions, like heat, currents, or limited resources, which can test your endurance and problem-solving abilities. Despite these challenges, the rewards of working directly in coral restoration - witnessing coral colonies grow and witnessing the resurgence of marine life - can provide deep personal satisfaction and a sense of accomplishment.

In the long run, these internships can significantly enhance your career prospects in marine science and conservation. The hands-on experience you gain, coupled with the opportunity to work closely with marine professionals, will make you a strong candidate for future job roles or advanced studies. Additionally, the connections you make with local conservation groups can lead to future job offers or collaborative opportunities. By participating in fieldwork internships, you not only contribute to vital conservation efforts but also lay the foundation for a successful career in marine conservation.

Notes, Thoughts, Ideas, etc.

University Research

University research internships focusing on coral reefs offer students an incredible opportunity to dive deep into marine science while gaining valuable hands-on experience. Many universities with marine biology or environmental science programs collaborate with coral restoration organizations, government agencies, and NGOs, giving students access to cutting-edge research projects. These internships often allow students to engage in real-world studies, from monitoring coral health and biodiversity to analyzing the impact of climate change on reef ecosystems. By applying for these research internships, you can immerse yourself in fieldwork that directly contributes to coral conservation.

One of the key benefits of a university-affiliated internship is the support and resources available to you. Many universities have partnerships with coral restoration projects, marine research institutes, and even international programs. As a student, you often receive access to the equipment, lab spaces, and mentorship that are crucial for conducting high-quality research. Additionally, the academic framework of these internships can help you earn credit toward your degree, further strengthening your academic and professional path. These experiences can also provide access to faculty guidance, networking opportunities, and recommendations that will be valuable in your future career.

Applying for university research internships focused on coral reefs also allows you to explore different aspects of marine science. Depending on the focus of the internship, you could be involved in various types of research, such as coral genetics, reef ecology, water quality testing, or restoration techniques. These internships are often multi-disciplinary, allowing you to integrate skills in biology, chemistry, data analysis, and environmental policy. This broad exposure can help you discover your specific interests within marine science and better inform your career choices post-graduation.

Participating in these internships can also be a great way to build a strong professional network. Collaborating with experienced marine scientists, graduate students, and conservationists can open doors to future research opportunities, jobs, or advanced study programs. Many interns go on to publish papers or present their findings at conferences, which is a great way to get recognized in the field. Whether you're pursuing a career in academia, environmental consultancy, or field-based coral restoration, university research internships provide an invaluable foundation that will set you on the right path toward a career in marine science.

Notes, Thoughts, Ideas, etc.

Marine National Parks

The aim of a National Marine Park is to connect people with the sea. Just like a National Park on land, their purpose is to enhance wildlife, conserve cultural heritage and promote public understanding, access and enjoyment. As an intern, you'll be involved in various activities aimed at restoring and protecting these delicate ecosystems. Interning at a marine national park offers a unique opportunity to contribute directly to the conservation and restoration of coral reefs. This hands-on experience allows you to actively participate in efforts that help revive damaged reefs while learning about the challenges faced by marine conservationists.

One of the key benefits of interning at a national park is the exposure to a multidisciplinary approach to coral reef restoration. Marine national parks often operate under strict environmental guidelines, ensuring that restoration efforts are conducted sustainably and in coordination with other conservation activities. As an intern, you'll gain insights into how coral restoration projects are integrated into larger conservation strategies, such as habitat protection, sustainable tourism, and climate resilience initiatives. You may also have the opportunity to collaborate with park rangers, marine biologists, and environmental educators, broadening your understanding of how coral reefs fit into the overall health of marine ecosystems.

While the experience is rewarding, interning in a marine national park can be physically and mentally challenging. The work often involves long hours in the sun or water, performing physically demanding tasks such as coral planting or monitoring reef conditions. Additionally, living in remote areas may require adapting to basic accommodations and limited access to modern amenities. However, these challenges are balanced by the unique opportunity to work in a protected marine environment, where you'll witness firsthand the beauty and biodiversity of coral reefs. The sense of accomplishment that comes from contributing to the preservation of these ecosystems makes the experience deeply fulfilling.

Beyond the personal satisfaction, an internship at a marine national park can significantly enhance your career prospects in environmental conservation or marine biology. The practical skills and knowledge you gain from working in coral reef restoration are invaluable when pursuing jobs in conservation, research, or park management. Moreover, being part of a national park's conservation team can connect you with a network of professionals and experts in the field, opening doors to future opportunities. Whether you're interested in scientific research, conservation policy, or marine education, this internship experience is a strong foundation for a career dedicated to protecting the world's oceans.

Notes, Thoughts, Ideas, etc.

Policy

Policy internships focused on ocean conservation provide an invaluable opportunity to delve into the intersection of environmental science, governance, and law. Interning with organizations that prioritize ocean policy allows students and emerging professionals to gain a practical understanding of how policies shape efforts in marine conservation, including the restoration of coral reefs. These internships typically involve engaging with experts in environmental law, policy analysis, and advocacy, offering hands-on experience in drafting proposals, conducting research, and analyzing regulations that impact ocean health. For those passionate about protecting marine ecosystems, these internships are a pathway to influence future legislation and policies in meaningful ways.

In the context of coral restoration, understanding the legislative and regulatory framework is essential. Through policy internships, interns can explore how national and international laws can be crafted and enforced to support the recovery of these ecosystems. Interns often work on initiatives related to marine protected areas (MPAs), fisheries management, and the implementation of sustainable coastal development policies. These experiences equip interns with the tools to advocate for stronger environmental protections and contribute to the design of policy measures aimed at mitigating coral reef degradation.

Policy internships also provide insights into the challenges and complexities of implementing ocean conservation policies. Laws and regulations often require balancing competing interests such as economic development, local livelihoods, and environmental sustainability. Interns learn how to navigate this landscape by collaborating with various stakeholders, including government agencies, NGOs, and local communities, to develop solutions that are both scientifically sound and politically feasible. This experience cultivates a deep understanding of the political and socio-economic factors that influence environmental decision-making.

Ultimately, internships in ocean policy foster a unique skill set for those interested in a career in marine conservation or environmental law. By focusing on coral restoration, interns can directly contribute to projects that have tangible environmental impacts while building a network of professionals dedicated to safeguarding marine biodiversity. These internships not only offer a platform to advocate for policy changes but also to develop leadership skills, critical thinking, and a comprehensive understanding of how policy frameworks can be leveraged to achieve conservation goals.

Notes, Thoughts, Ideas, etc.

International Marine Science

International marine science internships that focus on ocean conservation and coral restoration offer invaluable opportunities for students, researchers, and enthusiasts to engage with global environmental challenges. These programs are often based in diverse marine ecosystems, allowing participants to gain hands-on experience with critical conservation efforts aimed at protecting oceanic biodiversity. As oceans face increasing threats from climate change, pollution, and overfishing, internships in this field provide a platform to study the effects of these threats and contribute to sustainable solutions. The interdisciplinary nature of marine science enables interns to work alongside marine biologists, ecologists, and oceanographers, gaining a holistic understanding of marine conservation.

Coral restoration is a key area of focus within these internships, given the alarming rate at which coral reefs are degrading worldwide. Interns typically engage in various restoration techniques such as coral gardening, where fragments of coral are grown in nurseries and later transplanted onto damaged reefs. These efforts are crucial as coral reefs are essential to marine life, providing habitats for about 25% of all marine species. Interns not only learn about the biological and ecological processes involved in coral reef health but also participate in community outreach programs to raise awareness about the importance of coral conservation. This hands-on experience is essential for understanding the complexity of coral ecosystems and the urgent need for restoration.

These internships are often located in regions with high coral diversity, such as the Caribbean, Southeast Asia, and the Pacific Islands. This geographical focus allows participants to immerse themselves in unique marine environments and understand the local and global challenges faced by coral reefs. Many programs partner with local governments, NGOs, and research institutions, creating a collaborative environment where interns can contribute to ongoing scientific research and conservation initiatives. Interns also gain exposure to cutting-edge technologies used in coral monitoring, restoration, and marine data collection, further enhancing their skill set and career prospects in marine science.

In addition to scientific work, international marine science internships emphasize the importance of education and advocacy in ocean conservation. Interns often work with local communities, schools, and eco-tourism projects to promote sustainable practices and conservation awareness. This dual focus on scientific research and public engagement ensures that interns develop a well-rounded understanding of the complexities involved in marine conservation and coral restoration. By the end of their internship, participants not only contribute to tangible restoration efforts but also become advocates for ocean conservation, equipped with the knowledge and experience to inspire change on both local and global scales.

Notes, Thoughts, Ideas, etc.

Public Aquariums

Interning at a public aquarium that focuses on coral restoration offers an incredible opportunity to contribute to marine conservation efforts while gaining hands-on experience. As an intern, you would likely assist in caring for corals, monitoring their health, and learning about various restoration techniques such as coral gardening and fragmenting. This experience not only deepens your understanding of marine biology but also gives you practical skills in aquarium management and coral care.

One of the most rewarding aspects of interning at an aquarium with a coral restoration program is participating in research and conservation initiatives. You may work alongside scientists and marine biologists to study the effects of different environmental factors on coral health or help document coral growth and resilience. This research is crucial for improving restoration techniques and understanding how corals can adapt to changing conditions. By assisting in these projects, you directly contribute to efforts aimed at saving coral reefs, which are some of the most endangered ecosystems on the planet.

In addition to the scientific work, an internship at a public aquarium also involves educating the public about the importance of coral reefs and the threats they face. Through interactive exhibits, guided tours, and outreach programs, you would help raise awareness about marine conservation. Communicating scientific knowledge in a way that engages the public is a valuable skill that interns can develop, allowing you to inspire others to take action in protecting marine ecosystems. This aspect of the internship allows you to combine your passion for science with advocacy, making a tangible difference in conservation efforts.

Overall, an internship at a public aquarium focused on coral restoration is an enriching experience that blends scientific research, hands-on coral care, and public education. It provides a platform to contribute to critical conservation work while developing a broad range of skills, from marine biology techniques to communication and outreach. This opportunity not only advances your career in marine science but also empowers you to play an active role in the preservation of coral reefs for future generations.

Notes, Thoughts, Ideas, etc.

Chapter Three
Educational Opportunities

Educational opportunities in coral restoration provide a meaningful pathway to make a lasting impact on the health of our oceans while opening doors to exciting careers in marine science and conservation. For individuals who have already volunteered or completed internships, pursuing further education is a natural next step. Advanced learning in coral restoration can deepen your understanding of coral biology, restoration techniques, and the intricate dynamics of marine ecosystems. These educational programs are available at different levels, from short certification courses to full academic degrees in marine biology, environmental science, or conservation. These programs equip you with the knowledge and tools to engage in more specialized and impactful coral restoration efforts.

For those looking to expand opportunities beyond volunteering and interning, formal education in coral restoration can significantly enhance your skill set. Graduate programs, for example, often incorporate both fieldwork and research components, allowing students to contribute to scientific knowledge while developing practical skills in reef restoration. By studying topics such as coral genetics, climate change impacts, and advanced restoration methodologies, you position yourself as an expert in the field. This expertise can open doors to leadership positions within conservation organizations, government agencies, or academic institutions, where you can make a more profound difference on a larger scale.

As you pursue advanced education and training in coral restoration, you'll be adding valuable skills to your resume. Many programs focus on hands-on experience, giving you the opportunity to participate in restoration projects that involve cutting-edge techniques like coral gardening, outplanting, and monitoring reef health using scientific tools. Additionally, soft skills such as teamwork, communication, and problem-solving are honed through collaborative fieldwork.

Employers in marine conservation, research, and environmental consulting highly value candidates with this combination of technical knowledge and field experience, making your resume stand out in a competitive job market.

However, pursuing educational opportunities in coral restoration can be challenging. The field often requires a mix of academic rigor and physical stamina, especially for those working in field-based programs. You might find yourself working long hours in unpredictable conditions, conducting underwater research, or analyzing complex data. Funding for some educational programs or research projects can also be limited, which means you may need to seek scholarships, grants, or other financial support. Despite these challenges, the skills and knowledge you gain through these experiences will be crucial for overcoming real-world obstacles in coral conservation.

Despite the challenges, the journey is ultimately rewarding. The more specialized your education becomes, the greater your capacity to contribute to meaningful coral restoration efforts. You'll be equipped to work on advanced projects that address critical issues such as coral bleaching, reef degradation, and ocean acidification. In addition to the personal satisfaction of contributing to the protection and restoration of coral reefs, you'll have the chance to collaborate with leading experts, work on innovative solutions, and witness the positive outcomes of your efforts in real-time.

Pursuing education in coral restoration helps you network with professionals in the field, opening doors to career opportunities that might not have been available through volunteering alone. Many programs involve partnerships with NGOs, government agencies, and research institutions, giving you the chance to build connections that could lead to full-time job offers or further research opportunities. Whether it's working on international conservation projects, leading local reef restoration programs, or contributing to policy initiatives, the network you develop during your education can greatly enhance your career trajectory.

Having formal education and experience in coral restoration also makes you a strong candidate for leadership roles in the field. As the global demand for coral conservation grows, professionals with the right qualifications and experience are needed to lead projects, manage teams, and develop strategies for large-scale restoration efforts. Whether you aim to run your own coral restoration organization or contribute to marine policy, your educational background will provide the expertise required to lead effectively and make strategic decisions that impact entire ecosystems.

Pursuing educational opportunities in coral restoration is an investment in your future and the future of our planet. Not only does it provide the specialized skills and knowledge necessary to make a lasting difference, but it also enhances your career prospects and positions you to achieve your dream job in marine conservation. The combination of technical expertise, field experience, and the personal fulfillment that comes from contributing to coral reef recovery makes this path deeply rewarding. You'll have the chance to turn your passion for marine life into a lifelong career, making a real difference for future generations. So let's dive into some Educational Opportunities…

Notes, Thoughts, Ideas, etc.

Coral Restoration Workshops

Attending coral restoration workshops can be a valuable way to enhance your education and deepen your understanding of coral reef ecosystems. These workshops are often led by experienced scientists, conservationists, and restoration experts who provide hands-on training in the latest techniques and technologies used in coral restoration. By participating, you gain practical skills such as coral fragmenting, nursery management, and monitoring techniques. The immersive nature of these workshops allows you to apply classroom knowledge to real-world situations, enhancing both your expertise and your confidence in the field.

Workshops are also excellent opportunities to build your professional network. They bring together individuals from diverse backgrounds, including marine scientists, conservationists, volunteers, and policy makers. By attending, you can meet like-minded professionals and foster relationships with people who share your passion for coral restoration. Networking at these events could lead to future collaborations on projects or research, as well as introductions to potential employers or mentors. These connections can be invaluable as you progress in your career, providing opportunities for knowledge exchange and career development.

In addition to skill-building and networking, coral restoration workshops can also help you discover new career opportunities. Many workshops are hosted or supported by organizations that actively seek to hire skilled professionals or interns for ongoing projects. Attending workshops puts you on the radar of these organizations and allows you to showcase your skills and enthusiasm in person. You might find out about new job openings, internships, or collaborative research projects that you wouldn't have encountered otherwise. Engaging in these events demonstrates your commitment to the field and could give you an edge in the competitive marine conservation job market.

Attending workshops also shows your dedication to continuous learning, which is highly valued in the field of coral restoration and conservation. As new methods and technologies evolve, staying informed and up-to-date through these hands-on learning experiences signals to potential employers that you are committed to advancing your skills. This proactive approach to professional development can open doors to leadership positions, research opportunities, and other career advancements, making workshops an essential tool for both personal growth and career success.

Notes, Thoughts, Ideas, etc.

Marine Science Degree Programs

Pursuing a Marine Science degree is an excellent way to deepen your understanding of the marine environment while advancing your career in fields like coral restoration, marine biology, and conservation. These degree programs typically cover a wide range of topics, including oceanography, marine ecosystems, conservation biology, and marine policy. Through this curriculum, you'll gain a strong foundation in both the theoretical and practical aspects of marine science. This knowledge will not only prepare you for specialized work in coral restoration but also equip you to tackle other critical issues facing our oceans, such as climate change and biodiversity loss. A marine science degree can also give you a rounded understanding of oceanic processes; for example, understanding marine chemistry topics can show how nutrients in the water impact corals and ecosystems. Everything is connected.

In addition to academic learning, Marine Science degree programs provide numerous networking opportunities. Universities and research institutions often collaborate with marine conservation organizations, government agencies, and NGOs, giving you the chance to connect with professionals already working in the field. Many programs offer internships, research projects, and fieldwork opportunities where you can work alongside experienced marine scientists and conservationists. These experiences allow you to build valuable relationships that can open doors to future job offers, collaborative projects, or research grants, significantly boosting your professional network.

Marine Science programs also offer ways to enhance your practical skills and hands-on experience, which are critical for a career in marine conservation. Many degree programs emphasize experiential learning, with field-based courses that teach you skills like underwater research, coral monitoring, and data analysis. You may also have the opportunity to conduct your own research or work on restoration projects, gaining real-world experience that enhances your resume. Employers in marine science and conservation highly value candidates with both academic credentials and practical experience, so a Marine Science degree can give you a competitive edge in the job market.

Overall, earning a Marine Science degree is a significant step toward advancing your career in marine conservation. It not only strengthens your academic background and expertise but also provides essential networking and career development opportunities. By combining your degree with prior volunteer or internship experiences, you'll position yourself as a well-rounded candidate capable of making meaningful contributions to marine science, coral restoration, and broader environmental initiatives. The skills, connections, and qualifications you gain will be invaluable as you work toward your long-term career goals in marine science and conservation.

Notes, Thoughts, Ideas, etc.

Online Coral Restoration Courses

Online coral restoration courses offer a flexible and accessible way to deepen your understanding of marine conservation while advancing your career. These courses are designed to provide in-depth knowledge about coral ecosystems, restoration techniques, and the threats facing reefs, all from the convenience of your home. Whether you're a beginner or someone with prior experience, online courses allow you to study at your own pace, making them ideal for busy individuals or those unable to attend in-person programs. As more organizations emphasize the importance of coral restoration, having formal education through online courses can give you a solid foundation in the science behind coral conservation.

Enrolling in an online coral restoration course significantly adds to your education by covering both theoretical and practical aspects of coral biology, restoration methods, and the latest research in the field. These courses often include modules on coral anatomy, reproduction, and threats such as climate change and ocean acidification. Additionally, you'll learn about various restoration techniques, including coral gardening, artificial reefs, and innovative technologies used to monitor coral health. Many online courses are created by experts in marine science, giving you access to high-quality, up-to-date content that can strengthen your knowledge base.

Online coral restoration courses also provide opportunities to enhance your resume. Certifications from reputable courses show potential employers that you are committed to your professional development and passionate about marine conservation. Whether you are pursuing a career in marine biology, environmental consulting, or working with NGOs, having specialized certifications in coral restoration demonstrates a dedication to advancing your skills in this specific area. This added expertise can make you a more competitive candidate for jobs and internships, particularly for roles focused on marine ecosystems and conservation.

Online courses help you advance your career by offering valuable networking opportunities. Many courses are connected to marine conservation organizations or universities, giving you the chance to engage with instructors and peers who share your interests. These connections can lead to future collaborations, internships, or job opportunities. As coral restoration continues to grow as a field, having formal training from an online course positions you to take on more advanced roles, whether in research, project management, or fieldwork, ultimately helping you achieve your career goals in marine conservation.

Notes, Thoughts, Ideas, etc.

Join Reef Monitoring Programs

Joining Reef Monitoring Programs can offer significant benefits for anyone looking to advance their education and career in marine conservation. These programs provide hands-on experience in tracking the health of coral reefs, which can deepen your understanding of marine ecosystems and sharpen your practical skills. As a participant, you'll likely be involved in collecting data on coral cover, fish populations, water quality, and other critical indicators of reef health. This field-based learning helps you apply scientific methods in real-world scenarios, reinforcing what you may have learned in the classroom and expanding your knowledge of marine biology, ecology, and conservation strategies. This could even lead to becoming part of a published scientific study, which is a tremendous resume builder!

One of the most important benefits of reef monitoring programs is the opportunity to enhance your skill set. Reef monitoring requires the use of specialized equipment, such as underwater cameras, GPS systems, and data collection tools. You'll also learn valuable techniques like species identification, survey methods, and data analysis, which are essential for assessing the health of coral reefs. By developing these technical skills, you make yourself a more competitive candidate for jobs in marine science and conservation. Many employers in these fields look for individuals with experience in environmental monitoring, so participating in a reef monitoring program can set you apart from other applicants.

In addition to building practical skills, reef monitoring programs allow you to gain experience working in a team environment, often collaborating with marine scientists, conservationists, and fellow volunteers. This collaboration teaches you how to communicate effectively, manage projects, and solve problems in dynamic settings—valuable skills that are transferable to various careers in marine conservation, environmental consulting, or scientific research. Many reef monitoring programs also offer opportunities to network with professionals in the field, opening doors to internships, research positions, and long-term career opportunities.

Finally, participating in reef monitoring programs adds considerable value to your resume and professional development. By including this experience on your resume, you're demonstrating to potential employers or academic institutions that you have firsthand experience in marine fieldwork, data collection, and environmental assessment. These programs often involve certifications or training that can further boost your qualifications, making you a stronger candidate for advanced positions or educational opportunities. Whether you're just starting your career or looking to take the next step, reef monitoring experience provides a strong foundation for continued growth in the field of coral conservation and marine science.

Notes, Thoughts, Ideas, etc.

Coral Spawning Events

Participating in coral spawning events offers a unique and valuable opportunity for anyone pursuing a career in marine science or coral restoration. These events, where corals release eggs and sperm into the water for reproduction, are rare and fascinating natural phenomena. Being involved in coral spawning provides hands-on experience in one of the most critical aspects of coral reproduction and restoration. For students, volunteers, and professionals, it's a chance to witness this process firsthand, participate in the collection and study of coral larvae, and gain a deeper understanding of coral reproductive cycles. This specialized knowledge can significantly enhance your educational background, making you more knowledgeable in the field of marine biology.

The skills developed during coral spawning events are highly valuable in both research and restoration contexts. You'll have the chance to work closely with marine biologists, researchers, and conservationists, learning techniques for collecting, fertilizing, and transplanting coral larvae. These skills are essential for coral restoration, particularly in efforts that aim to increase genetic diversity and restore damaged reefs. Mastering these techniques can be crucial in advancing your coral conservation expertise, whether you plan to focus on scientific research or practical restoration work in your future career.

Adding coral spawning experience to your resume can set you apart in the competitive marine science and conservation job market. Employers in research institutions, NGOs, and government agencies look for candidates who have direct experience in coral restoration projects, and participating in coral spawning events demonstrates your commitment to the field. The technical skills, data collection experience, and teamwork you develop during these events are highly transferable to other areas of marine conservation, making you a stronger candidate for a wide range of positions, from research assistantships to project management roles.

Beyond the technical skills, coral spawning events are often a networking opportunity with professionals and experts in the field. Working side-by-side with established researchers and marine conservationists allows you to build connections that could lead to future job opportunities or collaborative projects. These relationships can be key to advancing your career in coral restoration, giving you access to a network of mentors and peers who can guide and support you as you move forward in the field. Overall, participating in coral spawning events is an enriching experience that boosts your education, skills, and career prospects while allowing you to contribute to the preservation and restoration of coral reefs.

Notes, Thoughts, Ideas, etc.

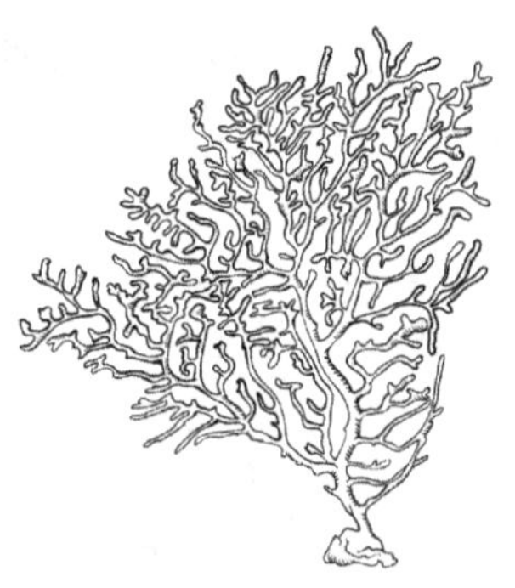

Attend Marine Conservation Conferences

Attending Marine Conservation Conferences offers numerous benefits for anyone passionate about coral restoration or marine conservation. One of the biggest advantages is the opportunity to network with professionals, experts, and like-minded individuals in the field. Conferences are often attended by marine biologists, conservationists, policymakers, and representatives from NGOs and academic institutions. These events provide a platform to meet people who share your interests, discuss the latest developments in coral restoration, and exchange ideas. By building these connections, you can open doors to future collaborations, job opportunities, or even research partnerships that can enhance your role in marine conservation.

Beyond networking, conferences offer valuable educational opportunities. Presentations, workshops, and panel discussions allow you to stay updated on cutting-edge research, restoration techniques, and emerging technologies in marine conservation. You can learn from experts who are leading the charge in coral restoration, whether they're discussing innovations in coral propagation, reef monitoring, or climate adaptation strategies. These learning experiences help expand your knowledge base and keep you informed on the latest trends in the field. This deeper understanding can prove invaluable when you return to your work or studies, as it enables you to apply new ideas and practices to real-world conservation efforts.

Attending marine conservation conferences can also significantly enhance your resume and career prospects. Participating in these events demonstrates your commitment to staying engaged with the latest developments in your field, which is a quality employers value. Presenting a poster or giving a talk at a conference also adds a prestigious accomplishment to your resume, showcasing your ability to contribute to academic and professional discussions. Even if you're attending as a participant, adding conference attendance to your resume highlights your continuous learning and professional development, which can make you a more competitive candidate for jobs, internships, or academic programs.

These conferences provide a space to advance your career in a strategic way. Whether you're looking for job opportunities, mentorship, or guidance on the next steps in your career, marine conservation conferences put you in touch with people who can help you reach your goals. Conversations with industry leaders and experts can offer career advice, introduce you to potential employers, or inspire you to pursue new avenues in marine conservation. By attending these events, you are positioning yourself within a global community of conservation professionals, expanding your reach and impact in the field.

Notes, Thoughts, Ideas, etc.

Study Abroad Programs

Participating in coral restoration study abroad programs offers an incredible opportunity to gain hands-on experience while expanding your understanding of marine ecosystems. These programs immerse you in real-world coral conservation efforts, often in regions rich with biodiversity, such as the Great Barrier Reef in Australia or the Coral Triangle in Southeast Asia. By working directly in the field, you not only gain practical skills in coral restoration techniques like coral gardening and transplantation but also learn about the cultural and ecological challenges that vary from region to region. This real-world experience helps to solidify concepts learned in the classroom and gives you a global perspective on coral conservation.

One of the greatest benefits of studying coral restoration abroad is the chance to advance your knowledge through exposure to diverse marine environments and restoration techniques. Different regions face unique environmental stressors such as ocean acidification, overfishing, or pollution, and being part of a study abroad program allows you to observe how these challenges are addressed in various parts of the world. By learning different restoration methods - from coral nurseries to artificial reef construction - you build a versatile skill set that can be applied in a range of global conservation efforts. This broadened perspective can also inspire innovative approaches to coral restoration in your future work.

The career advantages of participating in a coral restoration study abroad program are substantial. These programs not only enhance your technical skills but also make your resume stand out to potential employers. Being able to demonstrate international experience shows that you can adapt to new environments and work effectively in diverse teams. Many study abroad programs also provide opportunities to network with marine scientists, local conservationists, and global experts, which can lead to internships, research positions, or job offers. The relationships you build during your time abroad can be invaluable as you progress in your career, opening doors to even more collaborations and employment opportunities.

Besides the professional and academic benefits, the personal rewards of study abroad programs are also significant. You gain confidence from overcoming challenges in unfamiliar environments, learn about new cultures, and develop a deeper connection to marine conservation by witnessing firsthand the beauty and fragility of coral reefs. This experience not only enriches your understanding of coral ecosystems but also fuels your passion for preserving them. The combination of practical experience, global exposure, and personal growth that comes from a coral restoration study abroad program positions you for long-term success in marine conservation and helps you make a lasting impact on the health of our oceans.

Notes, Thoughts, Ideas, etc.

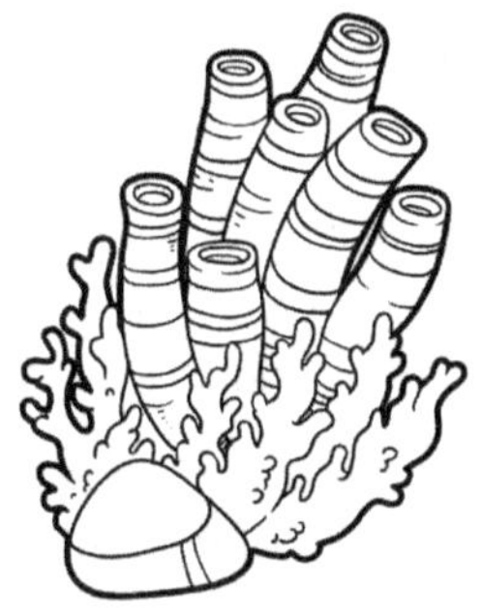

Coral Reef Field Schools

Attending and participating in Coral Reef Field Schools is a transformative experience that offers invaluable hands-on learning in marine science and coral restoration. These field schools take education beyond the classroom, immersing students in real-world coral ecosystems where they can apply theory to practice. By working directly on coral reefs, participants gain a deeper understanding of marine biology, coral ecology, and conservation techniques. This firsthand experience is crucial for developing the skills necessary to address the complex challenges that coral reefs face, such as climate change, pollution, and overfishing. Engaging with these environments provides a powerful learning experience that is impossible to replicate through books or lectures alone.

Field schools also allow students to work alongside leading experts in marine science, providing opportunities for mentorship and networking that can significantly advance your career. The chance to learn directly from marine biologists, conservationists, and restoration practitioners is invaluable. These experts often share their cutting-edge research, latest methodologies, and real-world problem-solving strategies, helping participants build a solid foundation for their careers. Additionally, the collaborative nature of field schools fosters strong professional connections with both peers and mentors, which can lead to internships, job offers, or further research opportunities.

Participating in coral reef field schools also helps students build essential practical skills that are highly valued in marine science and conservation careers. You'll gain experience in techniques such as coral transplantation, reef monitoring, species identification, and underwater data collection. These hands-on experiences not only boost your confidence but also enhance your resume, making you a more competitive candidate for positions in coral conservation, marine research, and environmental management. Employers in these fields often look for candidates with direct field experience, and attending a field school provides exactly that, giving you a clear edge in the job market.

In addition to technical skills, coral reef field schools instill a deeper passion and commitment to marine conservation. Being immersed in these fragile ecosystems reinforces the urgency of protecting coral reefs and motivates participants to take action in their future careers. Field schools offer a unique perspective on the global importance of coral reefs and the direct impact individuals can have in restoring and preserving them. This sense of purpose, combined with the knowledge and skills gained, empowers participants to contribute meaningfully to coral conservation efforts and set the stage for a fulfilling and impactful career.

Notes, Thoughts, Ideas, etc.

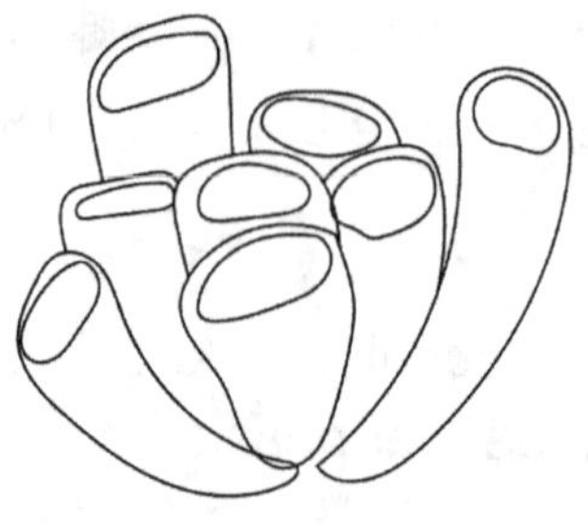

Citizen Scientist Expeditions

Participating in Citizen Scientist Expeditions for coral restoration offers a unique opportunity to combine education with hands-on environmental action. These programs allow volunteers to work directly on restoring coral reefs, learning about marine ecosystems, conservation efforts, and the science behind coral health. You'll receive training from marine biologists and experts, gaining a deeper understanding of oceanography, reef biology, and the environmental challenges coral reefs face. This is a powerful educational experience, giving you practical skills and knowledge that not only enhance your personal growth but also strengthen your resume, particularly if you're pursuing a career in marine science, conservation, or sustainability.

Citizen Scientist Expeditions also serve as excellent resume builders. Engaging in coral restoration highlights your commitment to environmental stewardship, teamwork, and problem-solving skills. Whether you're a student looking for fieldwork experience or a professional wanting to transition into environmental sciences, participation in such programs adds significant weight to your credentials. It shows prospective employers that you're proactive, resourceful, and willing to contribute to global conservation efforts, which are highly valued traits in today's job market. Additionally, the scientific and technical aspects you engage with during the expeditions can open doors for more specialized roles in research, fieldwork, and policy-making.

However, these expeditions aren't just about learning and working. They also offer the chance to experience an adventurous vacation while contributing to a meaningful cause. Many of these programs are set in tropical locations with beautiful coastlines and clear waters, allowing you to snorkel, dive, and explore vibrant marine environments as part of your work. You'll experience the thrill of working on the front lines of conservation while enjoying the natural beauty and adventure that comes with traveling to remote, exotic locations. This balance of adventure and purpose makes the experience fulfilling both personally and professionally.

Incorporating such an expedition into your career path can be a game-changer. It offers you a break from the typical vacation, turning it into something that nurtures your professional and personal growth. You'll return not only with enhanced skills and new experiences but also with a sense of achievement, having contributed to the protection and restoration of the planet's vital ecosystems. By aligning your adventurous spirit with your career aspirations, you create a narrative that shows you are both passionate and driven, qualities that can set you apart in competitive career fields.

Notes, Thoughts, Ideas, etc.

Diving Courses

Diving courses for coral restoration are becoming increasingly popular as you seek to play an active role in protecting marine ecosystems. These specialized courses teach you how to safely conduct underwater work aimed at rehabilitating and restoring coral reefs, which are vital to ocean health. The courses are often designed for scuba divers, ranging from beginner to advanced levels, and provide essential skills in underwater biology, ecology, and coral transplantation techniques. You gain hands-on experience in coral propagation, identifying and treating diseased corals, and monitoring restoration projects.

A major benefit of these courses is the educational value they provide. You both learn diving techniques and gain in-depth knowledge of coral ecosystems, their importance, and the threats they face, such as climate change and pollution. These courses often incorporate lectures, workshops, and field training led by marine biologists and conservation experts. This educational approach helps raise awareness about ocean conservation and equips divers with the tools needed to advocate for environmental protection long after the course has ended.

Moreover, completing a coral restoration diving course is an excellent addition to your resume. If you are pursuing a career in marine biology, environmental science, or conservation, this certification provides a practical, hands-on experience that sets you apart from others in the field. It demonstrates a commitment to environmental stewardship and shows that you have both the technical diving skills and the knowledge required to contribute to restoration efforts. Employers and research institutions value such qualifications, making it a beneficial step for your career development.

As well as the personal and professional benefits, diving courses for coral restoration contribute directly to the global effort to protect and restore coral reefs. The knowledge and skills gained allow you to assist in long-term restoration initiatives, helping to preserve biodiversity and mitigate the effects of human activities on these fragile ecosystems. This not only helps restore coral reefs but also supports the many marine species that depend on these habitats, ensuring the health of the ocean for future generations.

Notes, Thoughts, Ideas, etc.

Chapter Four
Hands-on Conservation Projects

Participating in hands-on coral conservation projects offers a unique opportunity to acquire invaluable knowledge and skills while contributing to the creation of healthier ecosystems. Coral reefs, often referred to as the "rainforests of the sea," are vital to marine biodiversity. By getting involved in these projects, you gain a deep understanding of the fragile ecosystems that coral reefs support. You learn about the delicate balance between marine species, their habitats, and the environmental factors influencing coral health. This hands-on experience goes beyond theoretical knowledge, providing direct insight into the challenges coral reefs face, such as climate change, pollution, and overfishing.

One of the primary benefits of engaging in coral conservation is the development of practical skills in marine biology and conservation science. Whether you are planting coral fragments, conducting surveys, or collecting data on coral health, these activities help you become proficient in scientific methods and research techniques. You'll also gain expertise in using specialized tools and technologies, such as underwater cameras, dive gear, and reef monitoring equipment. These skills are highly transferable to various career paths in environmental science, marine biology, and conservation.

Coral conservation projects often involve working with interdisciplinary teams, which helps you develop strong collaboration and communication skills. You will interact with marine biologists, environmental engineers, government officials, and local communities, fostering a collaborative mindset that is essential in conservation work. The ability to effectively work in teams and communicate findings to different stakeholders is a critical skill for any career in ecosystem management or environmental policy.

In addition to technical skills, hands-on coral conservation fosters problem-solving abilities. Coral reefs face complex issues that require innovative solutions. Through these projects, you learn how to assess environmental problems, design conservation strategies, and implement effective restoration techniques. This practical experience in troubleshooting and decision-making prepares you for real-world challenges in conservation and environmental management, making you more adaptable and resourceful in your career.

Moreover, coral conservation projects immerse you in the field, allowing you to witness firsthand the impact of human activities on marine ecosystems. This direct exposure strengthens your environmental advocacy and motivates you to pursue a career focused on sustainability. You become more aware of the broader environmental issues, such as ocean acidification, rising sea temperatures, and habitat destruction, which can shape your professional goals towards addressing these global challenges.

Participation in coral conservation also strengthens your network within the environmental field. You build connections with experts, researchers, and professionals who share your passion for protecting marine ecosystems. These relationships can open doors to internships, job opportunities, and collaborations on future projects. Having a strong professional network is vital for career advancement in the competitive field of environmental conservation.

Furthermore, the hands-on experience gained through coral conservation projects can significantly enhance your resume. Potential employers in conservation, environmental policy, and research look for candidates who have practical experience in the field. Demonstrating your active involvement in restoration projects shows your commitment to environmental stewardship and your ability to apply scientific knowledge to real-world problems.

Engaging in coral conservation projects also gives you a sense of purpose and fulfillment. Knowing that your efforts contribute to restoring and protecting coral reefs provides personal satisfaction and reinforces your commitment to a career dedicated to creating a healthier ecosystem. This passion and dedication are essential qualities for staying motivated on a career path in environmental conservation, ensuring that your work makes a tangible, positive impact on the planet.

Notes, Thoughts, Ideas, etc.

Control Invasive Species

Controlling invasive species like the lionfish is essential to protect coral reefs, which are vital ecosystems for marine biodiversity. Lionfish, originally from the Indo-Pacific, have invaded the Atlantic and Caribbean regions, threatening the delicate balance of these environments. Their rapid reproduction and lack of natural predators allow them to spread uncontrollably, preying on small fish and invertebrates that are crucial to the reef's health. By removing lionfish, we can reduce the pressure on coral reefs and give native species a chance to recover, maintaining a balanced ecosystem.

Coral reefs depend on a diverse community of organisms for their survival. Native herbivorous fish play an essential role in grazing algae that could otherwise overgrow and smother corals. However, lionfish prey on these smaller fish, reducing their populations and indirectly causing algae to proliferate. This leads to a decrease in coral health and resilience, especially as they face other stressors like climate change and pollution. Controlling lionfish populations helps ensure that these key species continue to support coral reefs by keeping algae in check and promoting coral growth.

Another benefit of controlling invasive species is the potential for long-term ecological restoration. Coral reefs are already under threat from ocean acidification and rising temperatures, which weaken their ability to recover from damage. By removing or reducing the number of invasive species like lionfish, we can create conditions that enhance the natural resilience of the reefs. In the absence of heavy predation from lionfish, native fish populations can flourish, contributing to a more vibrant and diverse ecosystem that is better equipped to withstand environmental challenges.

In addition to ecological benefits, controlling invasive species like lionfish can have significant economic and social impacts. Coral reefs provide food, income, and recreation for millions of people worldwide. Healthy reefs support fishing industries, attract tourism, and protect coastal areas from storms by acting as natural barriers. By helping to control the spread of invasive species, we can preserve these benefits for local communities and future generations, ensuring that coral reefs remain a valuable resource both environmentally and economically.

Notes, Thoughts, Ideas, etc.

Building Artificial Reefs

Assisting with projects that build artificial reefs offers a unique opportunity to gain hands-on experience in environmental conservation, marine biology, and sustainable development. Artificial reefs are structures placed in marine environments to promote marine life, enhance biodiversity, and support ecosystems that have been damaged or degraded. Participating in such projects can help develop a strong understanding of marine ecosystems, environmental restoration, and the technical aspects of constructing artificial habitats. These experiences can make you a valuable asset in fields related to environmental science, marine conservation, and ecological engineering.

Working on artificial reef projects helps you build essential skills such as project management, teamwork, and problem-solving. These projects often involve collaboration with scientists, engineers, divers, and policymakers, providing opportunities to learn how to coordinate multidisciplinary teams. You'll also gain experience in dealing with logistics, planning, and regulatory aspects of environmental projects. Being part of such efforts can sharpen your ability to manage complex projects while considering environmental sustainability and community engagement—skills that are highly valued in industries like environmental consulting, non-profit organizations, and government agencies.

From a technical standpoint, working on artificial reef projects enhances your understanding of marine technology and construction techniques. Whether it's placing reef structures, monitoring marine life recovery, or using underwater surveying equipment, the practical experience gained can give you a competitive edge in fields such as marine engineering or environmental monitoring. Furthermore, you'll be exposed to the challenges of balancing human intervention with natural processes, equipping you with a nuanced perspective on how to design solutions that support both ecological resilience and human activity.

Career advancement in marine conservation, environmental management, or even coastal development can be significantly bolstered by such hands-on involvement in artificial reef projects. Employers often look for individuals who not only have theoretical knowledge but also real-world experience and a demonstrated passion for sustainability. Assisting in the construction and monitoring of artificial reefs allows you to demonstrate your commitment to environmental stewardship, making you a standout candidate for roles that require both expertise and a proactive, solution-oriented mindset.

Notes, Thoughts, Ideas, etc.

Coral Propagation

Assisting with coral propagation for future transplantation is a valuable endeavor that contributes to marine conservation efforts and the restoration of fragile ecosystems. Coral reefs are vital to the ocean's biodiversity, supporting a wide range of marine life. By participating in coral propagation, you gain hands-on experience with delicate marine organisms and acquire practical skills in reef restoration. This type of conservation work allows you to understand the challenges faced by coral ecosystems, such as bleaching and habitat degradation, while equipping you with the knowledge and techniques to help counteract these problems.

Coral propagation is an interdisciplinary task that combines biology, environmental science, and marine management. Assisting in this process gives you the opportunity to work with biologists, conservationists, and researchers. You will learn how to propagate coral fragments in nurseries, monitor their health, and prepare them for eventual transplantation onto degraded reefs. This requires meticulous attention to detail, problem-solving abilities, and a deep understanding of coral biology, all of which are transferable skills for a career in marine biology, conservation, or environmental policy.

In addition to technical skills, assisting with coral propagation helps you develop critical soft skills like teamwork, leadership, and project management. Coral restoration projects often involve collaborations across multiple sectors, including government agencies, NGOs, and local communities. Working on such initiatives enhances your ability to communicate effectively with diverse stakeholders and fosters a sense of responsibility toward environmental sustainability. These experiences not only build your professional network but also demonstrate your ability to manage complex projects—a key asset for career advancement in environmental or conservation-focused roles.

Coral propagation also allows you to engage in cutting-edge conservation techniques, which can position you as a leader in the field. As marine environments continue to face challenges from climate change and human activity, expertise in coral restoration is increasingly sought after. By mastering the techniques involved in coral propagation, you can offer a unique skill set to potential employers in academia, governmental bodies, or conservation organizations. This involvement will showcase your commitment to environmental stewardship and position you for future roles in conservation leadership.

Notes, Thoughts, Ideas, etc.

Coral Fragmentation Projects

Participating in coral fragmentation projects offers a unique opportunity to engage directly in hands-on marine conservation work. Coral fragmentation involves breaking pieces of coral from healthy colonies and replanting them in suitable environments to help regenerate damaged reefs. Joining these projects will allow you to both assist in the restoration of marine ecosystems and gain invaluable experience in coral rehabilitation techniques. This direct participation allows you to contribute to reversing coral reef degradation caused by factors such as climate change, pollution, and overfishing. As these ecosystems are essential for biodiversity and coastal protection, your involvement can help preserve them for future generations.

Learning coral fragmentation techniques is an enriching educational experience. You gain knowledge about coral biology, species identification, and the environmental conditions required for coral growth. These projects often provide training in the use of specialized equipment and techniques, such as underwater planting and monitoring. You'll also have the opportunity to collaborate with marine biologists and conservation experts, expanding your understanding of broader marine restoration efforts. This hands-on experience is vital for anyone looking to build a career in marine biology, ecology, or environmental science, as it provides practical skills that are highly sought after in these fields.

Coral fragmentation projects also allow you to develop a wide range of transferable skills. Working in the field often involves teamwork, problem-solving, and adaptability, as marine environments can be unpredictable. The ability to conduct underwater surveys, analyze data, and contribute to scientific reports enhances your research and technical expertise. Furthermore, participating in such projects demonstrates a commitment to environmental stewardship, which can be an asset when applying for grants, fellowships, or advanced academic programs. It also strengthens your professional network by connecting you with leaders in marine conservation, which can open doors to future job opportunities or collaborations.

From a career advancement perspective, involvement in coral fragmentation projects can be a significant differentiator. Many employers in conservation, government agencies, and research institutions prioritize candidates with real-world experience in habitat restoration. The technical and scientific skills gained through these projects are directly applicable to roles in conservation management, research, and policy development. Additionally, as the effects of climate change and environmental degradation become more pressing global concerns, professionals with hands-on expertise in coral reef restoration will be increasingly valuable, positioning you at the forefront of efforts to combat ecological crises.

Notes, Thoughts, Ideas, etc.

Restore Damaged Reefs

Restoring damaged coral reefs after storms, such as hurricanes, is a critical environmental effort that benefits marine ecosystems and coastal communities. Extreme weather events can devastate reefs, breaking apart coral structures, damaging habitats, and disrupting marine biodiversity. To counteract these effects, restoration initiatives involve transplanting healthy coral fragments, stabilizing reef structures, and managing the surrounding environment to promote natural recovery. These activities are often collaborative, requiring the expertise of marine biologists, conservationists, engineers, and volunteers working together to repair the delicate ecosystems that reefs support.

Joining efforts to restore reefs damaged by extreme weather presents a unique opportunity to make a direct impact on environmental conservation. It allows individuals to contribute to preserving vital marine habitats that support fisheries, tourism, and coastal protection. For marine scientists and environmental professionals, reef restoration offers hands-on experience with cutting-edge techniques such as coral gardening, artificial reef construction, and the use of marine robotics. Collaborating on these projects provides valuable fieldwork experience that enhances technical skills, teamwork, and problem-solving abilities in real-world situations.

For professionals aiming to advance their careers in marine biology, ecology, or environmental science, participating in reef restoration projects can open new opportunities. These initiatives are often supported by government agencies, NGOs, and academic institutions, providing access to a broad network of experts and potential employers. Gaining experience in reef restoration can set you apart in a competitive job market, demonstrating a commitment to conservation and a capacity for fieldwork under challenging conditions. The work also provides the opportunity to publish findings, contribute to global conservation research, and influence policy related to marine protection.

Additionally, reef restoration projects help professionals develop leadership skills by managing teams, coordinating with diverse stakeholders, and overseeing complex restoration processes. These skills are transferable across many roles in environmental science and conservation. Engaging in such impactful work not only advances your technical expertise but also broadens your career prospects, offering pathways into policy, academia, and international conservation organizations.

Notes, Thoughts, Ideas, etc.

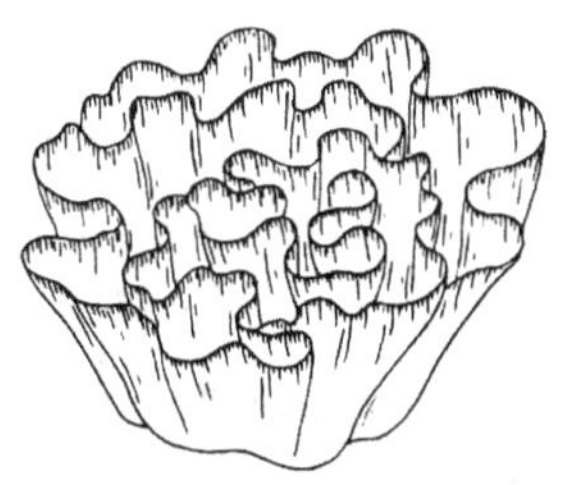

Coral Genomic Studies

Supporting coral genomic studies offers a unique opportunity to contribute to crucial research aimed at protecting coral ecosystems. Engaging in coral genomic studies gives you the ability to help identify resilient species or genetic variations that enable certain corals to withstand rising temperatures, ocean acidification, and other stressors. This research is essential for developing strategies to protect vulnerable coral species and promote the restoration of degraded reefs, ensuring the survival of these ecosystems and the biodiversity they support.

Getting involved in coral genetic research also provides a pathway to deepen your understanding of marine biology and genomics. This hands-on experience exposes you to cutting-edge techniques in DNA sequencing, bioinformatics, and evolutionary biology. You will learn how to analyze genetic data to identify coral species with traits that promote resilience to environmental challenges. participating in fieldwork or lab-based studies enhances your technical abilities and fosters problem-solving skills that are essential in scientific research. These experiences enrich your academic knowledge while equipping you with practical skills that can be applied across various scientific disciplines.

In addition to contributing to environmental conservation, coral genomic research can significantly bolster your resume and open doors to various career opportunities. Whether you aim to pursue a career in marine biology, environmental science, conservation, or biotechnology, participating in research projects demonstrates your commitment to important ecological issues. Employers and academic institutions value candidates with research experience, especially in emerging fields like genomics. Involvement in such studies shows your ability to work collaboratively on complex projects, apply advanced research techniques, and engage in innovative problem-solving.

Ultimately, by supporting coral genomic studies, you not only contribute to the conservation of fragile marine ecosystems; you also invest in your own professional growth. The skills and knowledge gained through this research are transferable to a variety of fields, from environmental management to academia. In fact, a lot of coral nurseries are already adapting these studies into the corals they raise in a coral nursery setting! Additionally, you will join a network of researchers, scientists, and conservationists who share your passion for preserving marine life. This network can provide mentorship, collaboration opportunities, and further career advancement, ensuring that your involvement in coral genomics has lasting benefits both for the planet and for your future.

Notes, Thoughts, Ideas, etc.

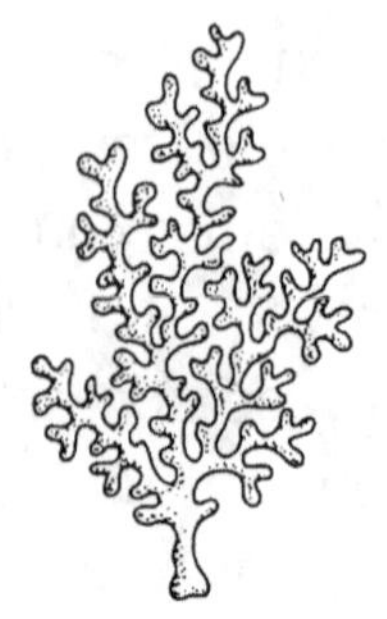

Coral Disease Management

Coral disease management is an essential aspect of marine conservation, particularly in addressing the alarming decline of coral reefs worldwide. Stony Coral Tissue Loss Disease (SCTLD) is one of the most significant threats to coral health, affecting a variety of species and leading to widespread mortality. To effectively combat this disease, it is crucial to implement monitoring programs that track the health of coral populations. This involves regular assessments of coral health, documenting disease prevalence, and identifying environmental factors that contribute to disease outbreaks. Individuals can gain valuable experience in field data collection, laboratory analysis, and the application of scientific methodologies to real-world challenges by participating in these monitoring efforts.

Engaging in coral disease management not only contributes to the health of marine ecosystems but also provides opportunities for skill development. As aspiring marine biologists or conservationists, working on projects related to SCTLD allows individuals to hone their research and analytical skills. They can learn about the ecology of coral reefs, familiarize themselves with disease identification protocols, and explore various treatment options, such as applying antibiotics or promoting microbial diversity. Additionally, involvement in community outreach and education initiatives can enhance communication skills, helping to bridge the gap between scientific research and public understanding of coral conservation issues.

Assisting in coral disease management initiatives can significantly bolster an individual's resume and career prospects. Employers in the fields of marine biology, environmental science, and conservation increasingly value hands-on experience and demonstrated commitment to ecological restoration efforts. Through participating in coral monitoring and management projects, individuals can showcase their dedication to marine conservation, problem-solving abilities, and teamwork skills.

Networking opportunities through collaborations with research institutions, NGOs, and government agencies can also lead to mentorship, internships, and potential job offers in the field.

Contributing to coral disease management, particularly in monitoring and managing SCTLD, is a multifaceted endeavor that offers personal and professional growth. As the health of coral reefs continues to decline, the demand for skilled professionals who can tackle these pressing issues is greater than ever. By actively engaging in this vital work, individuals can support the preservation of marine ecosystems and pave the way for a rewarding career in marine conservation. Fostering a deeper understanding of coral health and disease will be crucial in developing sustainable solutions to protect these invaluable resources for future generations.

Notes, Thoughts, Ideas, etc.

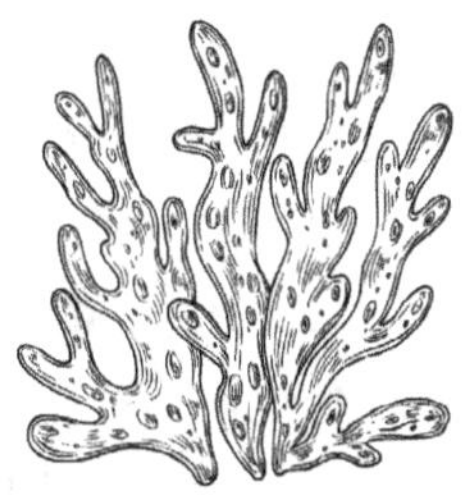# Transplant Corals to Reefs

Transplanting corals to reefs is an essential conservation strategy aimed at restoring damaged reef ecosystems. The practice of cultivating corals in nurseries and then transplanting them back to degraded areas has gained traction. This method not only aids in the recovery of reef structures; it also enhances biodiversity, improves ecosystem resilience, and provides crucial habitat for marine life. Selectively choosing coral species that are more resilient to changing environmental conditions means scientists and conservationists can bolster the chances of successful transplantation and long-term survival in the wild.

The process of transplanting cultivated corals involves several critical steps, including careful selection of healthy coral fragments, appropriate site assessments, and meticulous transplantation techniques. Coral fragments are typically grown in nurseries until they reach a suitable size for outplanting. Once ready, the corals are carefully attached to suitable substrates, such as rocks or reef structures, using biodegradable materials that minimize environmental impact. Successful transplantation requires knowledge of local marine conditions, including water temperature, salinity, and light levels, as well as an understanding of the biological interactions between corals and other reef inhabitants.

Besides enhancing reef health, participating in coral transplantation projects can significantly benefit individuals looking to advance their careers in marine conservation and ecology. Gaining hands-on experience in coral propagation, site assessments, and transplantation techniques both builds essential skills and enriches one's resume. Collaborating with marine scientists, conservation organizations, and community groups provides invaluable networking opportunities, fostering connections that can lead to future job prospects in environmental science, marine biology, and ecological restoration.

The successful transplantation of corals to reefs is a multifaceted effort that not only aids in restoring marine ecosystems but also serves as a pathway for personal and professional growth. Individuals can contribute to the resilience of coral reefs while enhancing their skill sets and career possibilities by engaging in this vital work. As the global community increasingly prioritizes marine conservation efforts, those with practical experience and expertise in coral transplantation will be well-positioned to lead initiatives that protect and restore these vital ecosystems for future generations.

Notes, Thoughts, Ideas, etc.

Long-Term Reef Monitoring

Volunteering for long-term reef monitoring is an incredible opportunity to contribute to the health of marine ecosystems while gaining valuable experience. Coral reefs are vital to ocean biodiversity and play a significant role in maintaining ecological balance. By participating in long-term monitoring projects, volunteers can engage in activities such as collecting data on coral health, assessing water quality, and recording biodiversity changes over time. This hands-on experience both enhances one's understanding of marine biology and helps develop essential research skills crucial for future career advancements in environmental science and conservation.

Long-term reef monitoring also allows volunteers to connect with experienced professionals and researchers in the field. This networking can lead to mentorship opportunities and valuable insights into various career paths within marine science and conservation. Volunteers often share their experiences and knowledge, enriching the overall learning environment and cultivating a strong network of like-minded individuals passionate about marine conservation.

Participating in these monitoring programs also plays a critical role in the broader fight against climate change and habitat destruction. Gathering long-term data allows volunteers to contribute to important research that informs conservation strategies and policy decisions aimed at protecting vulnerable coral reef systems. Their efforts can lead to better management practices and initiatives that enhance the resilience of reefs in the face of environmental challenges. This sense of purpose and impact can be incredibly fulfilling, motivating volunteers to continue their commitment to marine conservation long after their involvement in monitoring programs ends.

Engaging in long-term reef monitoring significantly enhances a volunteer's resume. The skills acquired through fieldwork, data analysis, and teamwork are highly transferable and sought after in many sectors, including environmental policy, marine research, and non-profit organizations. This experience bolsters academic qualifications and showcases a commitment to sustainability and conservation, traits that are increasingly valued in today's job market. By actively participating in these initiatives, volunteers can pave the way for future career opportunities while making a meaningful contribution to the health of our planet's oceans.

Notes, Thoughts, Ideas, etc.

Ecotourism Initiatives

Engaging in ecotourism initiatives offers a unique opportunity to explore the natural world while contributing positively to environmental conservation. Choosing to support ecotourism businesses focused on coral conservation means that individuals can not only enjoy the beauty of coral reefs but help protect these vital ecosystems as well. Coral reefs are crucial for marine biodiversity, serving as habitats for various species and providing resources for local communities. Participating in ecotourism initiatives can foster a deeper understanding of ecological challenges and inspire participants to advocate for sustainable practices that benefit both the environment and local economies.

Supporting ecotourism businesses that prioritize coral conservation often involves hands-on activities, such as snorkeling, diving, or participating in beach clean-up efforts. These experiences allow individuals to witness the vibrancy of coral ecosystems firsthand and provide a platform for education about the threats facing these habitats, including climate change, pollution, and overfishing. By engaging with local guides and conservationists, participants gain valuable insights into the importance of preserving marine biodiversity and learn about the specific initiatives being undertaken to restore and protect coral reefs. This knowledge can deepen one's commitment to sustainability and inspire further action in both personal and professional contexts.

In addition to the environmental benefits, engaging in ecotourism initiatives can significantly enhance one's skill set and career prospects. Many ecotourism programs offer training in areas such as marine biology, conservation techniques, and sustainable tourism practices. By actively participating in these initiatives, individuals can acquire practical skills that are increasingly desirable in various fields, including environmental science, tourism management, and education. Building a diverse resume through these experiences can open doors to future career opportunities, as employers often value candidates who demonstrate a commitment to sustainability and environmental stewardship.

Being a part of ecotourism initiatives not only supports coral conservation efforts but also cultivates a sense of global responsibility and awareness. As individuals engage in these activities, they become ambassadors for the environment, spreading knowledge and enthusiasm about the importance of protecting coral reefs and other natural ecosystems. Choosing to invest time and resources in ecotourism lets participants contribute to a sustainable future while enriching their own lives and career paths, fostering a profound connection with the planet and its invaluable resources.

Notes, Thoughts, Ideas, etc.

Chapter Five
Advocacy & Awareness

Advocacy and awareness campaigns are crucial components of coral restoration initiatives. They focus on educating the public, influencing policy, and fostering community involvement, ultimately leading to increased support for coral conservation efforts. Advocacy and awareness campaigns are essential for garnering public support and funding for restoration projects, ensuring the longevity of these critical ecosystems.

Advocacy efforts for coral restoration often involve collaboration among various stakeholders, including governments, non-profit organizations, research institutions, and local communities. Through raising awareness about the significance of coral reefs and the challenges they face, these campaigns can create a sense of urgency and responsibility among individuals and organizations. This collective action is necessary to influence policy changes, secure funding for research and restoration projects, and promote sustainable practices that protect coral reefs.

Community engagement plays a pivotal role in advocacy and awareness efforts for coral restoration. Local communities are often the first line of defense against environmental degradation, and their involvement is crucial for the success of restoration initiatives. Educational programs that involve hands-on activities, such as coral planting and monitoring, empower community members to take action and become stewards of their marine environments. These initiatives foster a sense of ownership and pride and help build a culture of conservation within communities.

Advocacy for coral restoration can create numerous career opportunities as well. As awareness of coral reef issues grows, so does the demand for professionals skilled in marine biology, environmental science, conservation policy, and community outreach. Organizations focused on coral restoration are often in need of experts who can design and implement effective programs, conduct research, and engage with the public. Additionally, job roles in education and communication are increasingly vital to disseminate information and foster public engagement.

Educational institutions can play a significant role in promoting coral restoration advocacy by integrating marine conservation topics into their curricula. Encouraging students to participate in research projects, internships, and volunteer opportunities related to coral restoration allows schools and universities to equip the next generation of environmental leaders with the knowledge and skills needed to address these pressing issues. This hands-on experience not both benefits students and contributes to the overall success of coral restoration efforts.

As more people become aware of the importance of coral reefs and the need for restoration, there is an increase in the potential for increased funding and support from both public and private sectors. This funding can be directed toward innovative technologies and research aimed at enhancing coral resilience and restoration techniques. Furthermore, successful advocacy campaigns can inspire individuals and organizations to take action, whether through financial contributions, volunteerism, or adopting sustainable practices in their own lives.

Advocacy and awareness for coral restoration are essential for the survival of coral reefs and the communities that depend on them. Through fostering public engagement and support, these efforts can create opportunities for career development while promoting sustainable practices and policy changes. As we collectively work towards restoring and protecting coral ecosystems, we ensure the health of our oceans in addition to the well-being of future generations.

Notes, Thoughts, Ideas, etc.

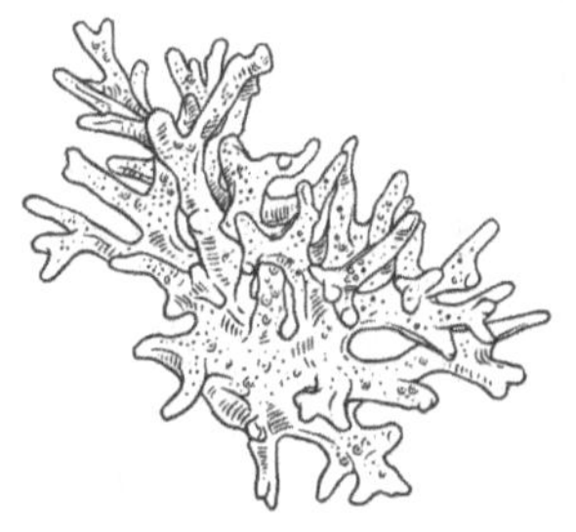

Coral Ambassador

Becoming a Coral Ambassador is an opportunity to champion the protection and restoration of coral reefs, ecosystems that are vital to marine life and the global environment. Coral Ambassadors actively promote awareness and conservation efforts, educate communities about the importance of coral reefs, and advocate for sustainable practices to protect these fragile environments. The role goes beyond simply spreading the message of conservation; it involves hands-on participation in initiatives like coral planting, research, and restoration projects. Ambassadors may work with NGOs, governments, and local communities to push for policies that ensure the long-term survival of coral reefs.

The importance of being a Coral Ambassador stems from the critical role coral reefs play in maintaining marine biodiversity. These ecosystems provide habitat and shelter to thousands of marine species, serve as barriers that protect coastlines from erosion and storms, and are integral to the livelihoods of millions of people worldwide. By becoming an advocate for their protection, Coral Ambassadors contribute to preserving biodiversity, sustaining food sources, and supporting the economic stability of coastal communities reliant on tourism and fishing industries.

Along with contributing to environmental preservation, becoming a Coral Ambassador can provide numerous opportunities for career development. Engaging in coral conservation efforts builds a diverse skill set, including environmental education, public speaking, project management, and community engagement. These skills are highly transferable to careers in environmental science, marine biology, policy advocacy, and sustainable business practices. Additionally, the experience of being part of international or local conservation networks enhances one's professional connections, opening doors to roles in NGOs, governmental organizations, and the private sector.

Coral Ambassadors often gain access to professional development resources such as workshops, conferences, and partnerships with scientific institutions. This allows them to stay informed about the latest research in marine conservation and to actively contribute to pioneering solutions for the environmental crisis facing coral reefs. By combining advocacy with career-oriented opportunities, being a Coral Ambassador not only serves the planet but also offers a meaningful path for individuals looking to align their careers with their passion for sustainability and conservation.

Notes, Thoughts, Ideas, etc.

Reef-Safe Sunscreens

Promoting reef-safe sunscreens is crucial for the health of our oceans and the preservation of marine ecosystems. Many conventional sunscreens contain harmful chemicals like oxybenzone and octinoxate, which have been shown to contribute to coral bleaching and damage. When these chemicals wash off our skin and enter the ocean, they can disrupt the delicate balance of coral reefs, leading to widespread coral mortality and impacting the entire marine food web. By advocating for sunscreens that are free from these harmful substances, we can protect these vital ecosystems and help ensure their longevity for future generations.

Choosing reef-safe sunscreens doesn't just benefit marine life; it also represents a growing opportunity for career advancements in the eco-conscious marketplace. As consumers become increasingly aware of the environmental impact of their choices, there is a rising demand for sustainable and reef-friendly products. Companies that prioritize the formulation and distribution of reef-safe sunscreens can attract environmentally conscious consumers, thus gaining a competitive edge. This shift toward sustainability can lead to job creation in research, product development, marketing, and sales as businesses expand to meet the needs of a more aware audience.

Promoting reef-safe sunscreens also offers a chance to educate the public about the importance of protecting coral reefs. By disseminating information about how everyday choices can impact the environment, we empower individuals to make informed decisions. This education can also inspire future generations to pursue careers in environmental science, marine biology, and conservation, further advancing the collective mission to protect our planet's oceans.

Advocating for the use of reef-safe sunscreens is not just about protecting coral reefs; it's about creating economic opportunities and fostering environmental awareness as well. Through the support of products that are free from harmful chemicals, we can contribute to the health of our oceans and promote sustainable practices that benefit both people and the planet. As we move toward a more sustainable future, embracing reef-safe sunscreens can play a vital role in ensuring the well-being of our marine ecosystems while opening doors for new career paths in an increasingly eco-conscious world.

Notes, Thoughts, Ideas, etc.

Coastal Communities

Working with coastal communities provides a unique opportunity to engage in meaningful volunteer work that promotes environmental sustainability while empowering local populations. These communities often rely on coral ecosystems for their livelihoods, making it crucial to educate residents about the importance of these ecosystems and the sustainable practices that can help protect them. Volunteers can facilitate workshops, training sessions, and community events aimed at raising awareness about the threats facing coral reefs. If volunteers share knowledge and resources, they can foster a collaborative environment where community members feel motivated to participate in conservation efforts.

One of the key benefits of volunteering in coastal communities is the chance to develop valuable career skills. Volunteers may engage in activities such as data collection, monitoring coral health, and conducting community outreach, which can provide practical experience in fields like environmental science, marine biology, and community development. These experiences can enhance resumes and help volunteers build a network of contacts within the environmental sector. As they work alongside professionals and community leaders, they gain insights into effective conservation strategies and sustainable practices that can inform their future careers.

In addition to skill-building, working with coastal communities offers the chance to make a tangible impact on both the environment and the lives of local residents. Sustainable practices, such as establishing marine protected areas, promoting eco-tourism, and encouraging responsible fishing methods, can lead to healthier coral ecosystems and improved economic prospects for communities. Volunteers can help implement these initiatives by collaborating with community members to develop strategies tailored to local needs and challenges. This collaborative approach promotes a sense of ownership among community members and ensures that conservation efforts are culturally relevant and sustainable in the long term.

Volunteering with coastal communities serves as a powerful catalyst for positive change. By educating residents about sustainable practices and working alongside them to implement these strategies, volunteers play a crucial role in preserving vital coral ecosystems. At the same time, they cultivate personal growth and professional development, making this volunteer experience mutually beneficial for both the communities and the individuals involved. Through dedicated efforts, volunteers can help pave the way for a more sustainable future, ensuring that coral reefs continue to thrive for generations to come.

Notes, Thoughts, Ideas, etc.

Marine Protected Areas (MPAs)

Advocating for Marine Protected Areas (MPAs) is essential for preserving vital ecosystems, particularly coral reefs, which are among the most biodiverse habitats on the planet. Coral reefs face numerous threats, including climate change, overfishing, pollution, and habitat destruction. Establishing MPAs can help mitigate these risks by creating safe havens where marine life can thrive, recover, and regenerate. By protecting these crucial environments, we support the survival of countless marine species and preserve the economic and recreational benefits that healthy reefs provide to coastal communities.

The campaign for MPAs should focus on raising public awareness about the significance of coral reefs and the challenges they face. This can be achieved through community engagement initiatives, educational programs, and partnerships with local stakeholders. Highlighting the ecological and economic value of coral reefs can cultivate a sense of stewardship among the public and motivate action toward the establishment of MPAs. Additionally, involving local communities in the decision-making process is vital to ensure that the designated areas address their needs and priorities while promoting sustainable practices.

Enforcement of MPAs is equally crucial for their success. Without proper management and monitoring, protected areas risk becoming ineffective due to illegal fishing, pollution, and other harmful activities. Advocacy efforts should include lobbying for adequate funding and resources for enforcement agencies, as well as the development of technology-based solutions for monitoring and surveillance. Training programs for local enforcement personnel and community members can also empower them to take an active role in protecting these vital ecosystems. By encouraging collaboration between government agencies, NGOs, and local communities, we can create a robust framework for the effective management of MPAs.

Advocating for MPAs presents an opportunity to build career skills and opportunities in marine conservation and sustainable management. As the demand for qualified professionals in marine science and ecology grows, creating and enforcing MPAs can serve as a springboard for careers in research, policy, and conservation management. Educational institutions and organizations can partner to develop training programs and internships that equip individuals with the necessary skills to contribute to marine protection efforts. By investing in human capital alongside environmental protection, we can create a future where both our oceans and the communities that depend on them thrive.

Notes, Thoughts, Ideas, etc.

Coral Bleaching

Coral bleaching is a critical environmental issue that arises when corals expel the symbiotic algae (zooxanthellae) living in their tissues, causing them to lose their vibrant colors and become white. This phenomenon is primarily triggered by rising ocean temperatures, which are closely linked to climate change. As global temperatures continue to rise due to human activities, such as burning fossil fuels and deforestation, the frequency and severity of coral bleaching events have increased dramatically. According to the National Oceanic and Atmospheric Administration (NOAA), coral reefs are experiencing unprecedented levels of bleaching, which not only threatens marine biodiversity but also the livelihoods of millions of people who depend on healthy coral ecosystems for food, tourism, and coastal protection.

Raising awareness about coral bleaching is essential for mobilizing action and fostering a deeper understanding of the implications of climate change on marine life. Social media platforms provide an effective channel for sharing information and engaging with diverse audiences. Individuals and organizations can highlight the beauty and importance of coral reefs, as well as the threats they face, by creating visually appealing posts, infographics, and videos. Additionally, sharing personal stories and experiences can humanize the issue, making it more relatable and compelling. Hashtags and campaigns can further amplify these messages, encouraging a broader community to join in the conversation and advocate for coral conservation.

Public speaking is another powerful avenue for raising awareness about coral bleaching. Whether in classrooms, community centers, or at environmental conferences, engaging in discussions about the science behind coral reefs and the impact of climate change can inspire listeners to take action. Effective public speaking conveys crucial information while cultivating skills like persuasion, confidence, and critical thinking. Addressing local issues related to coral bleaching and climate change allows speakers to connect with their audience on a personal level, prompting them to reflect on their own behaviors and consider how they can contribute to solutions.

Raising awareness about coral bleaching can open doors to various career opportunities in environmental science, marine biology, and public policy. As concern for the environment grows, there is an increasing demand for professionals who can communicate complex scientific information to the public and advocate for sustainable practices. Developing skills in social media communication and public speaking enables individuals to position themselves as knowledgeable advocates for coral conservation and climate action. Engaging in this vital work both contributes to the protection of marine ecosystems and advances personal and professional growth in an increasingly important field.

Notes, Thoughts, Ideas, etc.

Coral Restoration Funding

Coral restoration funding plays a vital role in the global mission to restore and protect some of the planet's most delicate marine ecosystems. Corals provide essential habitats for countless marine species and protect coastlines from erosion, making their health and survival critical to the broader ecosystem. Funding efforts aimed at coral restoration are particularly crucial in regions suffering from intense bleaching events, pollution, and overfishing. These areas, often concentrated in the Caribbean, Pacific Islands, and the Coral Triangle, face severe environmental pressures, making them high-priority zones for coral restoration initiatives. However, with adequate funding, it's possible to mitigate some of these impacts through active restoration projects, improved conservation practices, and public awareness campaigns.

One innovative funding strategy is crowdfunding, which allows individuals to make direct contributions to coral restoration projects. Crowdfunding platforms have seen success in recent years as they connect donors with meaningful conservation efforts. These platforms provide an opportunity for individuals from all walks of life to become involved, whether through small donations or larger contributions. Additionally, these platforms allow project managers to give live updates, report successes, and show progress, enhancing transparency and building trust with donors. This model of community-funded conservation allows for increased global engagement and can make a measurable difference, particularly in regions where local resources are scarce.

Corporate sponsorships and partnerships also play an essential role in funding coral restoration efforts. Many companies are now recognizing the importance of sustainable business practices and environmental stewardship. As part of their corporate social responsibility (CSR) efforts, companies can contribute to coral restoration projects, thereby enhancing their brand image while supporting an important environmental cause. Such partnerships can involve financial donations, but they might also include in-kind support like resources, equipment, or employee volunteer programs. Companies can also create initiatives such as "round-up" campaigns at checkout, where customers are encouraged to round up their purchases to the nearest dollar, with the extra funds going toward coral restoration efforts.

Government grants and international funding initiatives are fundamental to securing sustainable, large-scale coral restoration. National and regional governments often offer grants for conservation projects and can provide substantial resources for restoration efforts in collaboration with NGOs and local communities. International funding sources, such as the Global Environment Facility (GEF) or the United Nations Environment Programme (UNEP), offer substantial financial support to projects that have demonstrated potential for positive ecological impacts. Together, these diverse funding strategies can secure the financial support needed to protect and restore coral reefs in even the most vulnerable areas, ultimately ensuring these vibrant ecosystems remain a vital part of our planet's future.

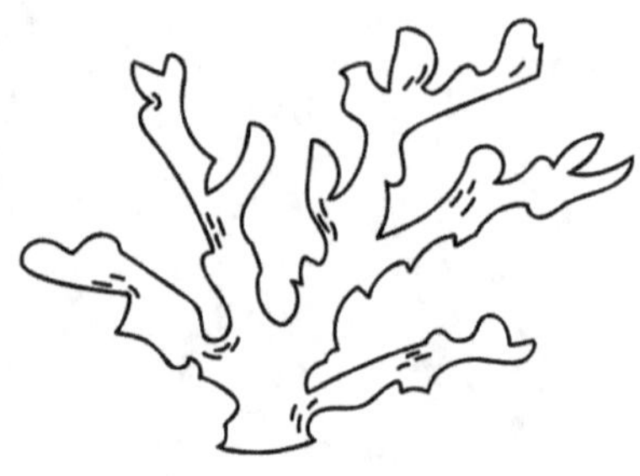

Write Articles on Coral Restoration

Writing articles on coral restoration is a powerful way to contribute to the global conversation surrounding coral conservation. By sharing knowledge and insights through blogs, magazines, or scientific journals, writers can highlight the critical importance of coral ecosystems and the challenges they face. Such articles can inform the public about the threats posed by climate change, pollution, and overfishing, while also showcasing successful restoration efforts. This both raises awareness and encourages readers to take action in their own communities, whether through advocacy, participation in local conservation projects, or simply making more environmentally conscious choices.

In addition to raising awareness, writing about coral restoration can help build a writer's career skills and reputation in the scientific community. Engaging in research and producing well-crafted articles fosters critical thinking, improves writing abilities, and enhances the writer's understanding of marine biology and ecology. Publishing in reputable magazines or journals establishes the writer as a credible voice in the field, opening doors to opportunities such as speaking engagements, collaborations with researchers, and participation in conservation initiatives. This visibility can be particularly valuable for students and early-career professionals seeking to make a mark in marine conservation.

The act of writing about coral restoration also promotes collaboration and knowledge sharing among stakeholders in the marine conservation community. By contributing articles, writers can connect with scientists, policymakers, and fellow advocates, forming a dialogue that leads to innovative solutions and partnerships. Highlighting ongoing research and case studies in restoration techniques can inspire others to adopt successful strategies in their own projects. These connections can strengthen collective efforts, ensuring that restoration initiatives are grounded in sound science and best practices, ultimately leading to more effective conservation outcomes.

Through articles, writers can inspire passion and commitment to coral restoration among diverse audiences. By weaving compelling narratives, sharing personal experiences, and showcasing the beauty and diversity of coral reefs, writers can engage readers emotionally, prompting them to care about these vital ecosystems. This emotional connection can drive action, whether through individual efforts or by influencing broader policy decisions. In this way, writing about coral restoration both informs and empowers individuals and communities to become stewards of the ocean, ensuring the longevity of coral reefs for future generations.

Notes, Thoughts, Ideas, etc.

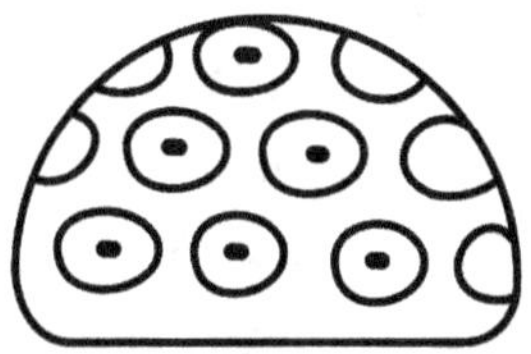

Coral Reef-Friendly Legislation

Supporting coral reef-friendly legislation is crucial in the fight against the degradation of these vital ecosystems. Coral reefs provide numerous benefits, including coastal protection, biodiversity support, and economic resources for local communities through tourism and fishing. Unfortunately, they are under constant threat from climate change, pollution, overfishing, and habitat destruction. By advocating for policies that protect these ecosystems, we can secure their preservation for future generations. Engaging in this legislative process helps safeguard coral reefs and creates a sense of community and shared responsibility among those who depend on these ecosystems.

Getting involved in local efforts can be a significant first step in advocating for coral reef protection. Many communities have initiatives aimed at promoting sustainable fishing practices, reducing plastic waste, and restoring damaged reefs. Volunteering with local organizations or participating in community clean-up events means individuals directly contribute to reef conservation and gain firsthand experience in environmental advocacy. These activities often lead to connections with like-minded individuals, cultivating a collaborative environment where ideas and strategies for effective legislation can be shared and developed.

At the national level, individuals can support initiatives that call for stronger regulations on pollution and fishing practices, as well as funding for coral reef research and restoration projects. Being a part of campaigns or writing to elected officials are ways concerned citizens can amplify their voices and influence decision-making processes. Additionally, joining advocacy groups dedicated to marine conservation can help individuals learn about current legislative efforts and effective advocacy strategies. These organizations often provide training sessions and resources that empower individuals to become effective advocates, helping them develop valuable skills in communication, negotiation, and public engagement.

On the international stage, coral reefs are a global concern that requires coordinated efforts across borders. Engaging with international treaties and agreements, such as the Convention on Biological Diversity, can create opportunities for individuals to contribute to global conservation goals. Attending international conferences or webinars focused on marine conservation allows advocates to learn from global experts, share local successes, and collaborate on larger initiatives. Involvement in these international efforts helps protect coral reefs and enhances one's reputation as a dedicated advocate for the environment, opening doors to further opportunities in conservation and community leadership. Through the support of coral reef-friendly legislation at all levels, individuals can play a crucial role in the fight to save these irreplaceable ecosystems.

Notes, Thoughts, Ideas, etc.

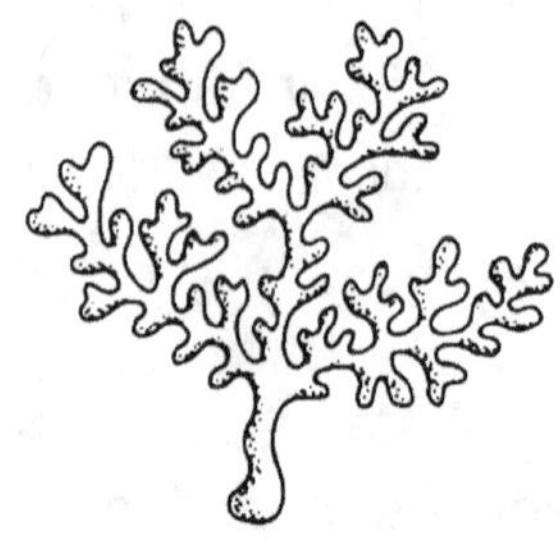

Environmental Education Programs

Hosting or participating in Environmental Education Programs focused on coral reefs is an impactful way to raise awareness about the importance of these ecosystems and inspire action toward their conservation. Whether you are leading school workshops, community events, or public lectures, these programs offer a platform to educate students and everyday people about the critical role coral reefs play in marine biodiversity, coastal protection, and the global climate system. Creating engaging and accessible content that explains complex topics like coral bleaching, overfishing, and ocean acidification can help attendees connect with the issue and understand the urgency of coral conservation. By organizing these events, you become a key player in fostering a more environmentally aware community.

The experience of hosting or participating in such programs is deeply rewarding and helps build valuable skills. You'll refine your public speaking abilities, learning how to communicate scientific concepts in a clear and engaging manner. Additionally, you'll improve your organizational skills as you plan events, coordinate with partners, and manage participants. Engaging with a variety of age groups and backgrounds sharpens your adaptability and ability to connect with diverse audiences. These skills are not just essential for advancing conservation efforts; they are also transferable to other areas such as project management, leadership, and community outreach.

Hosting environmental education programs also helps you build a positive reputation within your community. As someone taking an active role in educating others about the environment, you'll become a trusted source of knowledge and inspiration. Your work in spreading awareness can lead to partnerships with local schools, businesses, and environmental organizations, further increasing your impact. Over time, this visibility can lead to more opportunities, such as invitations to speak at larger events or collaborate on larger conservation projects. Your growing reputation as a leader in environmental education can also open doors for funding and support for future initiatives.

Environmental education programs play a crucial role in fostering a culture of stewardship and action within the community. By teaching people about coral reefs, you're not only informing them about an environmental issue; you're empowering them to take action. Whether it's through adopting sustainable practices, supporting conservation efforts, or pursuing careers in marine science, the knowledge they gain through these programs can lead to real-world impact. By participating in or leading these initiatives, you contribute to the long-term protection of coral reefs while also growing personally and professionally within the conservation field.

Notes, Thoughts, Ideas, etc.

# Local Government Collaboration

Working with local governments to implement coral conservation strategies offers a unique opportunity to engage in high-impact environmental work. Local governments play a crucial role in the protection and restoration of coral reefs by setting policies, enforcing regulations, and allocating resources for conservation efforts. As a collaborator, you can contribute to a wide range of initiatives, from establishing marine protected areas to developing sustainable coastal management plans. Public outreach is also a key component, where you can help raise awareness about the importance of coral reefs through educational campaigns, community events, and media outreach. This experience allows you to engage directly with local communities and decision-makers, creating a bridge between science and policy.

By working with governments, you gain valuable experience in the political and regulatory aspects of conservation. Understanding how environmental policies are created, enforced, and funded is crucial for advancing coral restoration efforts on a larger scale. You might contribute to drafting legislation that protects critical coral habitats or help design enforcement strategies for existing marine conservation laws. This experience provides insights into the complexities of balancing environmental protection with local economic and social interests. You'll develop skills in negotiation, advocacy, and policy analysis, all of which are highly sought after in the marine science and conservation fields.

Along with policy work, partnering with local governments on habitat protection projects offers hands-on experience in coral conservation. You may be involved in fieldwork initiatives such as coral outplanting, monitoring reef health, or conducting research on local marine ecosystems. Governments often work closely with NGOs, scientists, and community groups to implement restoration projects, giving you the chance to collaborate with a diverse range of stakeholders. This collaboration helps build your reputation as a knowledgeable and effective advocate for marine conservation, opening doors to future opportunities in both governmental and non-governmental sectors.

Through this work, you both gain practical experience and build a valuable reputation in the marine science advocacy community. Successfully contributing to government-led conservation efforts demonstrates your ability to work within larger systems and influence meaningful change. Your involvement can also lead to networking opportunities with influential figures in conservation, including policymakers, scientists, and community leaders. Building these relationships enhances your credibility and opens the door to leadership roles in future conservation initiatives, both locally and internationally. The skills and reputation you develop by working with local governments can significantly advance your career in marine science and advocacy.

Notes, Thoughts, Ideas, etc.

Now What?

Congratulations on reaching the end of this book and taking the time to learn about 50 impactful ways to make a difference in coral restoration and conservation! You have explored a wide range of strategies, from hands-on volunteering and participating in coral planting, to spreading awareness on social media, to advocating for policy change. These actions may seem small on their own, but collectively they contribute to a larger movement dedicated to protecting one of the planet's most precious ecosystems: coral reefs. Every effort counts, and by completing this book, you've already taken an important step toward becoming part of that global effort.

The knowledge you've gained empowers you to take action - whether it's getting involved with local reef restoration efforts, signing up for eco-volunteering trips abroad, or even just making everyday choices that reduce your carbon footprint and lessen your impact on the oceans. Coral reefs are facing unprecedented challenges due to climate change, pollution, and overfishing, but we have the tools and resources to help turn the tide. Now, more than ever, your commitment is needed to restore and preserve these vital ecosystems for future generations.

This journey doesn't end with the completion of the book. You now have the opportunity to take what you've learned and turn it into tangible action. Maybe you'll choose to join a coral nursery project, or perhaps you'll organize community clean-ups to reduce pollution in local waters. Whatever direction you take, remember that every effort makes a difference. By acting now, you're contributing to the solution, ensuring that coral reefs continue to thrive and support the incredible biodiversity of marine life that depends on them.

As you move forward, we invite you to explore the many additional resources and opportunities available on the Marine Science Odyssey website. Here, you'll find everything from in-depth articles and guides to educational videos and volunteer listings, all focused on coral restoration and marine conservation. Whether you're looking for more ways to get involved, want to connect with others in the marine science community, or are seeking further education opportunities, this platform will be an invaluable resource in helping you continue your journey toward making a lasting impact.

By completing this book, you are one step closer to becoming a champion of coral conservation. The skills and knowledge you've gained not only add value to your personal and professional life but also contribute to a larger global effort to protect the oceans. Marine ecosystems are in peril, but with dedicated individuals like you, there is hope. Your willingness to learn and take action means that you are part of the solution, and the marine science community is stronger because of your contribution.

We encourage you to share what you've learned with others. The more people who understand the importance of coral reefs, the greater the collective impact we can have. Educate your friends, family, and community about the need for coral conservation and inspire them to take action as well. Whether it's through personal conversations or spreading the word on social media, your voice can help raise awareness and motivate others to join the fight to save our reefs.

Remember, coral restoration is not a one-time effort; it's an ongoing process that requires continuous attention and action. Your journey doesn't stop here, and the impact you can make has no limits. As the challenges facing coral reefs continue to evolve, so too must our efforts to protect them. Stay engaged, stay informed, and never lose sight of the fact that your actions - no matter how big or small - are making a real difference in the world.

As you reflect on all you've learned and achieved, keep this quote in mind: "The greatest threat to our planet is the belief that someone else will save it." This is a reminder that each of us has a role to play in safeguarding our environment. Your dedication to coral conservation is not only inspiring but essential. Thank you for taking this journey, and we look forward to seeing the positive impact you will continue to make in the marine science community.

Notes, Thoughts, Ideas, etc.

About the Authors

Amber Lawrence

Amber Lawrence's journey to co-creating *"Coral, Conservation, & Careers: 50 Ways to Save the Reefs!"* is deeply rooted in her lifelong connection to the ocean and her unwavering dedication to marine conservation. Growing up in Florida, Amber was surrounded by the beauty of the ocean, and her father instilled in her a love for the underwater world at an early age. By the age of five, Amber was snorkeling, marveling at the vibrant marine life beneath the waves. At 15, she became a certified SCUBA diver, spending countless hours exploring Florida's coral reefs and gaining an appreciation for the delicate ecosystems that support such incredible biodiversity. These formative experiences laid the foundation for her passion and commitment to protecting the ocean.

Although Amber's life took her to the mountains of Colorado, the ocean's call was never far from her heart. Her annual SCUBA diving trips allowed her to experience the diversity of marine ecosystems worldwide while witnessing firsthand the devastating effects of climate change, pollution, and human impact on coral reefs. These trips deepened her understanding of the urgent need for conservation and reinforced her sense of responsibility to protect these ecosystems. Each dive became not only an adventure but a reminder of the critical work that needed to be done to preserve the ocean's beauty for future generations.

In 2017, Amber watched the documentary *Chasing Coral,* which became a turning point in her life. While she had already witnessed coral bleaching and degradation in Florida, the documentary illuminated the global scale of the crisis. Inspired and motivated, Amber began advocating for coral reef protection, raising awareness, and sharing her experiences to educate others about the importance of conservation. The film's message was a catalyst that drove her to take meaningful action, ultimately leading her to pursue a hands-on role in coral restoration.

At the age of 40, Amber made the life-changing decision to move to the Florida Keys, immersing herself fully in the world of marine conservation and coral restoration. She became an active volunteer, contributing her time to coral restoration projects, beach cleanups, and public awareness campaigns. Her work with organizations dedicated to reef restoration gave her firsthand knowledge of the challenges and triumphs involved in saving these ecosystems. Amber's dedication and drive to make a difference became her passion and the cornerstone of her contributions to *"Coral, Conservation, & Careers"*, ensuring this book is as actionable as it is inspiring.

Amber's unique background as a diver, volunteer, and advocate provided the perfect perspective for creating a guide that empowers others to take action. Her contributions to *"Coral, Conservation, & Careers"* reflect not only her experience but also her deep passion for sharing the tools and resources needed to protect coral reefs. Through the book, and her involvement with the Marine Science Odyssey, Amber hopes to inspire readers to embark on their own journeys in marine conservation, proving that even the smallest efforts can lead to monumental change for the health of our oceans.

Scott W. Gonnello

Scott W. Gonnello is an environmental entrepreneur with a deep passion for marine science and conservation. With decades of experience, Gonnello has built a career that merges his innovative business skills with his dedication to environmental causes. He has successfully founded and managed multiple companies, all while advocating for sustainability and ocean health. His ability to balance environmental goals with business acumen makes him uniquely qualified to helm Marine Science Odyssey, a project designed to inspire action and awareness in the science community by bringing everyone together more effectively.

Gonnello's work is driven by a love for the ocean and an understanding of the challenges it faces. His entrepreneurial spirit has led him to launch ventures that not only succeed commercially but also serve as platforms for raising awareness about environmental issues. Over the years, Gonnello has become known for his innovative approach to solving problems, particularly in areas related to sustainability. This background has provided him with a unique perspective, allowing him to lead Marine Science Odyssey with a mix of creative problem-solving and scientific understanding, essential for bringing the complexities of marine conservation to a broad audience.

In addition to his entrepreneurial achievements, Gonnello is a dedicated advocate for education and outreach. He has spent years connecting with communities, sharing the importance of marine science, and inspiring the next generation of scientists and conservationists. His commitment to fostering global partnerships has made him a sought-after figure in the marine science world, further solidifying his role as a leader capable of guiding both you and Marine Science Odyssey into new territories of exploration and collaboration.